Children with Special Needs

Assessment, Law and Practice –
Caught in the Acts

3rd edition

of related interest

Young Adults with Special Needs
Assessment, Law and Practice – Caught in the Acts
John Friel
ISBN 1 85302 231 4

Children with Special Needs

Assessment, Law and Practice –
Caught in the Acts   3rd edition

John Friel

Jessica Kingsley Publishers
London and Bristol, Pennsylvania

The right of John Friel to be identified as author of this work has been asserted by him in accordance with the Copyright, Designs and Patents Act 1988.

First published in the United Kingdom in 1991 by
Jessica Kingsley Publishers Ltd
116 Pentonville Road
London N1 9JB, England
and
1900 Frost Road, Suite 101
Bristol, PA 19007, U S A

2nd edition published 1993
3rd edition published 1995

1st edition copyright © 1991 Harry Chasty and John Friel
3rd edition copyright © 1995 John Friel

Crown Copyright is Reproduced with the
permission of the Controller of HMSO:

Codes of Practice in the Identification and
Assessment of Special Educational Needs
Extracts

How to Appeal
Extracts

Library of Congress Cataloging in Publication Data
A CIP catalogue record for this book is available
from the Library of Congress

British Library Cataloguing in Publication Data
A CIP catalogue record for this book is available
from the British Library

ISBN 1-85302-280-2

Printed and Bound in Great Britain by
Biddles Ltd., Guildford and King's Lynn

Contents

Chapter 1

A Guide to the Legal Rights of Children with Special Needs

When Harry Chasty and I first agreed that a book was needed in this field, our object was to inform parents, educational advisors, and lay advisors to parental organisations about parental rights. The book was written to describe as simply as possible the requirements of procedure and practice in this area. It was felt that a book that dealt with both the psychological principles (written by a psychologist), and guidance (by a lawyer) would be a new and exciting development.

In this third edition, the practical legal part of the book has grown to become a substantial book in itself. As a result of the 1993 Education Act, a guide to legal rights needs to stand on its own.

In practice, we have found that those who have found the book useful range from parents helping their own child, to lay advisors, psychologists, education officers, barristers and solicitors. It remains my intention to keep the book as simple as possible so that it can act as a guide to everyone from parents to lawyers.

Once again, the book approaches the subject from the point of view of a parent wishing to inform themself of their child's rights. The book is a practical guide, not a legal text book.

The 1993 Education Act substantially reforms the 1981 Education Act. It brings in a completely new system of appeals, namely an Independent Appeal Tribunal with a legally qualified chairman. The number of appeals has been expanded, covering many of the main defects in the 1981 Education Act.

The problems which caused public complaint under the 1981 Act particularly arose where parents did not have the right to appeal a refusal to assess a child. If an assessment started but was not completed the only appeal was in writing to the minister. Equally, there was no appeal against the request to reassess, where a state-mented child is not doing well enough, or against a decision to cease to maintain a statement, and this was a very major defect in the Act itself.

The appeals were to so called 'Independent Committees', which were, in practice, in some parts of the country packed with council-lors. Although in many areas the members did in fact try and be independent, in many other areas independence was in name only. Lastly, the appeal to the minister gave rise to considerable concern. In the first volume of this work, the minister's methods of dealing with Section 8 Appeals were justly and properly criticised. The system was, frankly, appalling.

This system was gradually reformed; in fact, it was improved enormously – effectively beyond recognition – and produced some well reasoned and fair decisions. Those who worked on the system undoubtedly produced substantial reforms, and the civil servants behind this reform did a very good job.

Nonetheless, the system itself had numerous defects and the Independent Appeal Committee, if it favoured the parents, was generally ignored on appeal to the minister. The system itself led to some curious decisions. There is little doubt that the minister was looking very critically at local education authorities and was consis-tently coming up with carefully reasoned and good decisions. How-ever, there continued to be, in a substantial minority of cases, very substantial errors.

The history of the Department for Education on judicial review, together with the Welsh Office, led to most challenges to ministerial decisions being conceded by the relevant government departments, and the only case fought in full was *R -v- The Secretary of State ex parte S*, due to be reported in 1995 Education Law Reports Part I.

Many of these defects, but not all, are now cured by the 1993 Education Act. In the old system, parents might have considered the use of the Education Reform Act Exemption Rights; these were very seldom used, and with the coming into force of the new Act these rights are virtually useless. A sensible new system with a neutral tribunal that can make binding orders upon the local education authority (LEA) has replaced it. It remains to be seen whether this system will become too legalistic, which would be a deterrent to parents with a very just and proper claim.

Effectively, there is no legal aid to cover those who are really poor but in need of considerable help. The Green Form Legal Aid system as presently constituted can be used to help to some degree, but there is a grave injustice in that if a parent wants to quarrel about whether their child should go on holiday they can get legal aid to go to the county court.

On the other hand, if a parent who has no means disputes the decision of the LEA in relation to the future of a child with special educational needs, they can get limited legal aid to cover a certain amount of preparation, but no legal aid to cover the cost of the case itself. These cases involve matters of enormous complexity, and great importance; this is hardly fair.

Part III of the 1993 Act continues the differentiation between children with statements of special educational needs and those children whom are helped in the ordinary school. By increasing the rights of appeal, which relate to assessment, and in relation to the statementing process, the Act also seeks to place a greater obligation on those responsible for children in the ordinary school.

The Act is also intended to ensure that a local authority has an up-to-date overall policy for children with special needs, and that it coordinates with the governing bodies of all schools in the area, and the Funding Council for grant maintained schools, and that the governing bodies of schools themselves do likewise.

The second major reform is the introduction of the Code of Practice by section 157 of the Act. The Code of Practice is an important new development in the Act. Local education authorities and all persons exercising functions under the Act must have regard to the Code as must the Appeal Tribunal in any appeal. The Code ought to have the effect of raising standards of provision and assessment for children with special needs nationally, increasing knowledge of the need for intervention and knowledge of how to support such children, ensure that there is greater help available and better identification procedures.

However, this is likely to be a gradual process, and there will still be cases where children need help, and are not getting adequate help unless they have a statement of special educational needs. The Code of Practice and a new Tribunal give rise to two potential problems.

The Code is a five stage assessment process, and one would hope that if it is apparent that the child's problems need immediate intervention, or that the parent has made out a reasonable case that the child's current school either is not capable of dealing with a child's problems or simply has not available the provision, the local education authority will in fact get on and assess the child's needs. If an over-legalistic interpretation is put upon the Code, however, it can take years to go through the first three stages. In a deserving case it is not the intention that children will suffer by delay.

Second, there is a danger with the tribunal (particularly where there is no legal aid), that there may be long legalistic hearings, which discriminate against all the parents (including those who can afford legal help); this would be a useful way for local education authorities to avoid paying for children with special needs.

These developments need to be watched carefully. The new Tribunal appears to be aware of this difficulty. However, the complexity and difficulties of these cases have been underestimated by the Department for Education (DFE) consultative document on the Tribunal.

It has to be said that the reforms which are in place in the Act represent, from the point of view of most parental organisations, a fairer deal for parents and children than the previous legislation. It is to be hoped that it works.

Finally, those who have read earlier editions of this book will be aware that the model of a child with special educational needs used by the authors has been a child with severe dyslexia.

This remains a model in the sample report (Appendix 3) because of the psychological input. It will remain the example in the present book. The legal principles and guidance in this book apply to all disabilities and are not limited to dyslexia. The example of the expert report (Appendix 3 to this book), which has been published in the last two editions, remains an example based on a severely dyslexic child. For all children with special educational needs, the pattern of this report on needs and provision is guidance to be followed in any case where dispute arises. It is therefore of general application.

Obviously, other psychologists have their methods, but unless a report follows the basic principle of dealing individually with each and every need, then addressing the point of provision, it is of little use to anybody. A defective report will be of little use to any lawyer, or Independent Legal Tribunal, if it fails to deal with the issues in the case.

Chapter 2

Identifying Children with Special Needs
Assessment

IS THERE A PROBLEM?

The parents of a child who believe that there is a problem will not normally think, does my child have a special educational need? It would be obvious to the parents, possibly to the child, and often to the teacher that something is wrong. The educational aspects of identification and assessment of children with special needs are obviously the province of education. At present we are solely concerned with the practical and legal means of recognition, where parents believe their child has not been picked up or, while the school appreciates that there is some problem, it has either got it wrong, or has failed to appreciate the extent of the child's difficulties.

Before a parent or an education authority can know whether or not there is a legal obligation to make provision under the Education Act 1993 for a child's needs, a child must first be assessed. The 1981 Act followed the policy of identifying a child, then assessing the needs, and thereafter making provision. The 1993 Act has reformed the statutory obligations, but adopts the same approach.

IDENTIFICATION OF CHILDREN WITH SPECIAL NEEDS

The LEA, by virtue of section 165, are required to exercise their powers with a view to securing or identifying those children who have special educational needs and for whom it is necessary for the authority to determine the special educational provision (section 165(1) and (2)). The meaning of the word 'necessary' is considered later in this work (see pp.12–13). This is a general statutory guide to practice; however, on the issue of a specific failure to identify a child's needs at all or completely, these powers are unlikely to be relevant to the individual case in hand.

Section 167 deals with assessments of children. Where the authority form the opinion that a child falls or probably falls within the following criteria:

1. Has special educational needs; *and*

2. It is necessary for the authority to determine the special educational provision which any learning difficulty he may have calls for.

The authority must serve a notice on the child's parents that they propose to make an assessment. Having served the notice, if they are still of the opinion that an assessment is necessary, they must make an assessment.

For those who are not subject to assessment or who have been assessed but who are not statemented, the duty to provide help lies on the school. In section 161 the duty is placed on the governing body of the school, whether it be grant maintained or maintained, save for maintained nursery schools which are directly governed by the local education authority. In these cases the duty is on the LEA or any governing body to use their best endeavours in exercising their functions in relation to the school to make sure that any registered pupil who has special educational needs is given the provision which his learning difficulty calls for (section 161(a)).

The duties on the governing body are increased under the 1993 Act. This is particularly due to the fact that (by section 161(5)) the governors are obliged to report on the implementation and effectiveness of the school's policy for pupils with special educational needs in their annual governors' report to parents. In this respect the Act also provides for regulations to be made by the Secretary of State. These regulations are the Education (Special Educational Needs) (Information) Regulations 1994, Statutory Instrument No. 1048 which provide for the publication by the governing body of information of matters set out in the schedule to the regulations.

The information required to be published is as follows:

1. Basic information about the school's special educational provision. This applies whether the school is a maintained school or a grant-maintained school.

2. The information must include the objectives of the governing body in making provision, the policy of the governing body, and how the policy will contribute towards meeting those objectives.

3. Full details of all the relevant staff with special educational needs (SEN) responsibility. This includes admission arrangements, and the type of provision available at the school, including any specialisations.

The information must also include published information and state how resources are allocated amongst pupils with special educational needs, how these are identified and their needs determined by the school, the school's arrangements for providing access to the National Curriculum, and arrangements in particular for the governing body to receive and deal with complaints from parents. The information published must also include information about the school's staffing policies and work with other bodies beyond the school such as the LEA's specialist staff, the social services and health authorities. This applies to both LEA maintained schools and to grant maintained schools.

This information must be published and made available to parents, the LEA, the district health authority and the funding authority, by the 1st August 1995. It must also be made available to prospective parents at the school (Regulation 3). The Annual Reports of the governing body must include details (by Regulation 5 and Schedule 4) of the success of the governing body's policy, since the last annual report, any significant changes in the policy, the allocation of resources among pupils with special needs and the outcome of any consultations held under section 161.

The overall effect of these changes is to make available to parents a great deal more information, and to enable parents and local education authorities to see what is actually being done by each ordinary school for pupils with special needs, what their policy is, and how the allocated funds are spent on such children.

These duties include a duty to secure that the responsible person, who is defined as the head teacher or a governor (i.e. the chairman of the governing body or a designated governor for the purposes of the Act or, in the case of a maintained nursery school, the head teacher), where the LEA has informed that person of a pupil's needs, ensures that they are made known to those likely to teach him. The governors are also required to secure that teachers in the school are aware of the importance of identifying and providing for those registered pupils who have special educational needs.

The Act continues the dual category of pupils with statements for whom the LEA make provision, and those without statements for whom the school makes provision. In each case an assessment may be necessary. In all statement cases an assessment is essential.

PREPARING A REQUEST FOR AN ASSESSMENT

If possible, a parent who can afford independent advice would be well advised to obtain it, even if the school wishes to have their child assessed, and supports the idea of an assessment or statement. An independent expert report is very useful, and certainly, if the school is not recommending an assessment, or agreeing that there is a problem, they are an essential aid to the parent.

Expert reports which do not address the issues are basically of no assistance to parents at all. The expert must now prepare a report on the basis of the Code of Practice. The Code is considered in Chapter 5. If the expert considers that the school cannot make provision from its own resources or simply that a child's needs are much more severe than can be normally dealt with without a statement of special educational needs, this must be clearly set out and justified in the report. Equally, if the school and the parents are in disagreement about the extent of the child's needs, or the school has refused to consider the child as having special educational needs, the expert may wish to consider including the parental account in their report. Equally, an expert who feels that this will compromise the neutrality of such a report must make it clear that the parents disagree with the school's views or request that the parents separately set out that issue, particularly if the parents are not intending to seek legal advice. For lawyers reading this part of the book, obviously if the parents are not happy with the approach of the school, or the school has simply not detected a problem, it is important that this fact be clearly stated in any letter requesting a statutory assessment.

THE NEED FOR ADDITIONAL REPORTS

Obviously, many children with special needs have conditions which require medical treatment or the oversight of doctors. In all such cases medical reports should be obtained. Where there is a need for reports on particular forms of support, particularly speech therapy, physiotherapy and occupational therapy, it is clearly important that an independent report is obtained, if that is possible.

Speech therapy in particular is often limited by health authorities to what they are prepared to provide rather than what the child needs. It is therefore important that parents who have children with such problems get proper professional advice identifying the extent of the problem, such as the speech problem and the necessity for specialist speech therapy, and liaison with the teaching staff. It is important, however, that any psychologist assessing the child with special educational needs draws the attention of the parents or professional advisors, such as solicitors of the parents, if they do not already appreciate it, to the need to obtain an independent report.

PSYCHOLOGIST'S REPORTS AND THE CODE OF PRACTICE

The last important requirement of an expert report is that it refers to the provisions of the Code of Practice. In reaching a decision as to whether this is a case that should be the subject of a parental request for an assessment, or in cases where psychologists may be consulted by the governing bodies of grant maintained schools under the provisions of either Sections 172 or 173, the expert must bear in mind the three stages of the Code of Practice which assume intervention by the school in such cases on a steadily increasing level. If the Code of Practice has not been applied or has been inadequately applied, or if there has been a complete failure to diagnose, the expert should advert to those matters. It is therefore important for an independent expert to be conversant with the Code of Practice, because certainly the local education authority will be. An expert whose report is deficient in this respect can expect to be criticised. Further, if the expert is to give evidence before the Independent Appeal Tribunal, the report that omits consideration of the Code of Practice is likely to be the subject of considerable criticism and very fruitful cross-examination by those representing a local education authority. Psychologists and advisory bodies would, therefore, be well advised to be very familiar with the provisions of the code of practice. Such knowledge is essential.

In reaching a decision as to whether an assessment is required under the Act by the local education authority, there is, however, a danger of the expert being over-cautious and dazzled by the provisions set out in the Code of Practice particularly where the child needs immediate help.

THE INTENTION OF THE ACT AND THE CODE OF PRACTICE

The intention of the Act and the Code of Practice is that children with special educational needs are provided, if possible, by their ordinary school with adequate help. If such help is not available or enough help is not available, or if the child needs extra specialist help or a specialist environment, then that provision should be made. The Act has tightened up the time limits, particularly those relating to assessment; it plainly does not intend for children with special needs to suffer unnecessarily. The expert ought to consider the following questions:

1. Is this a case where the child clearly needs extra provision, a statement, very specialised provision, or a specialist school?

2. What evidence is there that immediate intervention by way of an assessment is required?

3. Given the extent of the problems, is this the sort of difficulty for which one would expect an ordinary school to have provision readily available? Would one normally expect LEA intervention? Examples of this are children in an ordinary school who require speech and language therapy; for example where the difficulty is dyspraxia or hearing impairment.

4. If there is a different of viewpoint between the parents and the school, is there clear professional evidence, i.e., the results of psychometric testing which establishes, at least on the balance of probabilities, that the child is not slow to learn, or suffering from stress due to some family problem, but has a learning difficulty, which requires special educational provision?

5. Is there evidence of emotional problems, stress or illness interrelated with stress exhibiting itself, which shows that the child needs immediate assessment, and more help.

6. Every report must contain a list of the child's needs and the provisions to meet those needs.

In conclusion, the report by any advisor whether a psychologist, doctor or therapist employed by the parents, or indeed an LEA, should finish with a clear conclusion, if possible summarising the issues with details of the recommended provision. If an assessment or statement is needed, the report should say so.

Legal aid is not available in cases under the 1993 Education Act save under the Green Form Scheme. Therefore the parent will normally have to pay for the case privately. If means are limited, parents can obtain proper advice from a number of charities, local bodies and, in the case of a dyslexic child, the Dyslexia Institute or the British Dyslexia Association (there are local British Dyslexia Association branches all over the country). Appendix 7 provides sources of help and advice other than from the LEA.

THE WORD 'NECESSARY' WHICH APPEARS IN THE STATUTE AND THE EXPERT

As far as the expert is concerned, the existence of a statutory definition where an assessment is required, namely, that it is *necessary* for the LEA to determine the special educational needs, requires some comment at this point. If the expert has considered the matters set out above, the answer will be either that an assessment is not necessary due to the fact that the school can make provision or has actually made adequate provision, and the parent is wrong, or that it is necessary, either because the condition is too severe and the child needs extra help, or because the school has not until now, cannot or will not provide such provision without an assessment. The test the expert should bear in mind is that of practical reality; the legal test is the balance of probabilities. If, therefore, it is more probable than not that an assessment is necessary, the expert and the parents should advise and the parents should request such an assessment.

In relation to the Education Acts, the word 'necessary' was considered in the case of *R -v- Devon County Council ex parte G* 1989 1 AC pg. 573 when section 55 as amended of the Education Act 1944 was considered. This involves a local education authority which had to consider arrangements for the provision of transport or otherwise as they consider necessary...for the purpose of facilitating the attendance of pupils at schools.' At p. 604(E) to (F), Lord Keith of Kinkel defined 'necessary' in the terms of the definition of Lord Griffiths *in re*: An Inquiry under the Company Securities (Insider Dealing) Act 1988 I AC p.660, p.704(D). He said that Lord Griffiths, in a different context, para-phrased it as 'really needed', which Lord Keith stated is 'a helpful way of expressing a concept'. At pg. 604 (E) to (F) he made it clear it was for the authority to decide whether free transport is 'really needed'.

Applying this test to the case of a child with special needs, it is plainly for the authority initially on the facts of the case, and on Appeal, the tribunal on the facts of the case, to decide whether an assessment or a statement are really needed.

APPEALS IN GENERAL

The nature and number of appeals capable under the new Act are considered in a separate chapter. However, this chapter considers the issue of expert reports, which are likely to be used at all stages in the appeal. The expert should therefore bear in mind that the report should be a document clearly constructed, setting out the results clearly, and if possible in a manner which a lay parent and the Tribunal if necessary can read and understand, clearly setting out any relevant history, together with tests, providing details of needs and provision and coming to conclusions. The report will therefore need to address the subject of the dispute and reach a conclusion.

I would also consider that if the expert knows that the report is likely to be read by a Tribunal, he should seriously consider including personal details of their qualifications and experience as an appendix to any report or, in fact, as the introductory part.

Members of tribunals will be greatly assisted by the expert setting out in detail their qualifications in advance together with their experience, and expertise including contributions to relevant works, research or indeed any books written by them. In this context an expert can either set out, on every occasion, their details or provide a standardised appendix to be added to their report in the event of an appeal.

Chapter 3

Request for Assessment

ASSESSMENT PROCEDURE

There are two methods of starting the assessment procedure where the local authority fails to do so. The earlier Education Acts introduced the right of a parent to request an assessment of special educational needs under section 9 of the Act. The provisions of section 9 have been replaced by section 173 which is in substantially different terms. However, section 174 creates a new method of requesting an assessment. It solely applies to grant maintained schools where a section 13 direction has been made to admit the child. The 1993 Act therefore draws a distinction between LEA-maintained Schools, voluntary schools and grant-maintained. It is true that the Code of Practice does provide for school referral but it creates no mandatory statutory duty. So long as the requirements of sections 173 and 174 are satisfied, there is a mandatory statutory duty to assess where the child's parents request an assessment or where the governing body of a grant-maintained school request an assessment. The Code of Practice requires the LEA to have regard to its contents by section 157, but this does not require an assessment when there is a referral under the Code of Practice in the same way as Sections 173 and 174 approach an assessment.

In the case of a child at a grant-maintained school subject to a section 13 direction, so long as the parents and the school are not in dispute or the parents are not substantially critical about the school, it may be very advantageous if the parents can persuade the governing body to make a referral to the local education authority. On a practical basis this puts the child in a grant-maintained school on the same basis as a child referred by this school under Part III of the Code of Practice. Equally, the school may be only too pleased to make such a referral, because the school itself may have little available expertise or no expertise in the particular field, and would not in fact be able to provide adequate help without LEA intervention through a statement. If the parent has already obtained a detailed expert report which is accepted, or substantially accepted by the school all that need be done is for the parent, after a meeting with the head teacher, to agree with the head teacher or with the appropriate person on the governing body that the school will make such a referral.

For practical reasons the school may be greatly assisted by a statement, or at least by the assessment process, in that it will bring extra resources to the school or make available to the school expert knowledge which would not normally be available outside of the assessment process. It is therefore essential for grant-maintained schools to see that the statutory power is actually a great help to themselves and the child in that it is a key to extra resources which they could not normally provide to such children.

A parent has the right to use section 173 in all cases. For practical purposes it is a more powerful referral in all cases if it is a joint referral. In any event, the LEA must inform the child's head teacher that a request has been made under section 173 of the code of Practice (see Paragraph 3.16). Parents are well advised to lay the ground work in advance. If there is a dispute between the parent and the school and if section 173 (the right of parental request is chosen), it is important that the parent makes it quite clear what areas of dispute there are between themselves and the school where the parent feels the school has fallen down or failed to appreciate the child's problems fully.

Section 173 requires an authority to comply with a request for an assessment of the child's special educational needs under section 167 if there is no statement, or no assessment has been made within a period of six months prior to the request and:

> It is necessary for the authority to make an assessment under that section, 1731(c).

Where a parent is making a request under section 173, it should be accompanied by a letter from the parent enclosing, if possible, the expert report, and giving reasons. Those reasons should include, if there are disagreements with the school, an explanation of the parental views.

The LEA has a month to make a decision, and must inform the child's head teacher of the request, and ask the school for written evidence about the child, in particular the school's assessment of the child's learning difficulty and the school's account of the provisions which have been made. The Code of Practice requires that the psychology service and other bodies, such as the designated medical officer or social services, should be informed.

Where there is a referral by the governing body of a grant maintained school, it must be in the case of a child for whom a direction has been issued under section 13 of the Act to admit the child. The criteria for assessment are essentially the same, save for the fact a notice must be served on the child's parent as the parent requests an assessment under section 173:

1. A child has to have special educational needs.

2. The LEA must believe it is necessary to determine his special educational needs.

Again, a local education authority is required to serve a notice. This notice is to be served on a child's parents and that of the grant-maintained school.

CONTENTS OF NOTICES UNDER SECTIONS 173 AND 174

The requirements of the notices under sections 173(2) and 174(5) and (6) are slightly different. If there is a refusal, the LEA must give notice of the refusal to the parents, and in the case of a referral under section 174, to the governing body. In the case of section 173(2)(b) they are also required to give the parent notice of the right of appeal to the Tribunal also in the case of a referral by a grant-maintained school. If, however, the authority do decide to assess under section 174, they are under an obligation to give notice in writing both to the child's parents and the governing body of the decision and of their reason for making it.

THE DECISION TO MAKE AN ASSESSMENT

The relevant statutory wording is that it is necessary to make an assessment under section 167.

Section 167(1) states where a local education authority are of the opinion that a child for whom they are responsible falls or probably falls, in sub-section 2 below...the definition in section 167(2) is as follows:

1. The child has special educational needs

2. It is necessary for the authority to determine his special educational provision. The test is therefore that the child has or probably has a need for a statement.

CRITERIA FOR MAKING AN ASSESSMENT ON PARENTAL REQUEST

1. The Code of Practice, Chapter 3 paragraphs 19 and 20 deal with children who may need immediate referral for statutory assessment. This can be defined as follows:

   (i) Children may demonstrate such significant difficulties that the school may consider it impossible or inappropriate to carry out the full three stages of its assessment, i.e., they may have major sensory or other impairments which without immediate specialist intervention is beyond the capacity of the school and will lead to increased learning difficulties.

   (ii) In cases of obvious severe disability.

   (iii) Whether or not the child has gone through the three stage assessment processes set out in the Code of Practice, if the child probably falls or does fall within the criteria for a statement in the Code of Practice and irrespective of the assessment process in school, it is necessary to assess.

   (iv) Where the evidence points on the balance of probabilities to the fact that the school's approach has been wrong, or the child is developing greater learning difficulties despite the school's intervention, or in some cases lack of intervention.

   (v) Where a school has not the help available.

Particularly in the context of criterion (v) above, it should be remembered that the local education authority must form the view that the child probably falls within section 167(2). The test of this is the balance of probabilities, which is a relatively low standard, as the local education authority is entitled to commence an assessment and to decide not to make a statement by section 167(6). This does not mean that it is certain that a statement must be made nor that there is a high probability, only that it is more likely than not that a statement will result.

Further, as the Code of Practice concentrates solely on severe or complex learning difficulties, it must be remembered that it ignores the fact that some children may have learning difficulties which are significant and may not be severe or complex but may well be beyond the capacity of an ordinary school. In addition, some ordinary schools simply will have no such capacity. It may well be that the ultimate outcome of an assessment would be a change of school, for example, to one in the local area with more provision. This is no reason for not making an assessment and, obviously in such circumstances, without a statutory assessment it is doubtful whether it can be certain a statement is unnecessary or that an appropriate decision is being made in relation to the child's needs.

CHILDREN WITH STATEMENTS

Where a child is the subject of a statement maintained under section 168 of the Act, a parent has a right to request further assessment in respect of the child under section 167 by reason of section 172(2). The LEA must be satisfied that it is necessary to make a further assessment under the section, and there must have been no assessment within a period of six months prior to the request section 172(2)(b).

Again, an appeal lies against a refusal to reassess the Tribunals (section 172(3)(e)). The LEA is required to give notice to the parent of the refusal.

In practical terms one would not expect a request to arrive within six months of the making of a statement save in exceptional circumstances. Where, however, it is apparent that the child's condition is worse than originally assessed, the condition has declined, or the provision is not working or working adequately, an assessment should be made. If there is disagreement about the rate of progress, the parent should support, if possible, such a request with at least one expert report checking all available evidence of progress or lack of it. If a report is not available, full reasons should be given. Where there is failure being experienced which is causing stress, anxiety or worse, a medical report should be obtained, particularly when consultations have taken place with general practitioners, or psychiatrists.

Chapter 4

The Statutory Duty to Make Provision for Children with Special Needs

The Education Act 1944 imposed a duty on the local education authority to assist children who required special educational treatment. The Education Act 1981, which came into force in 1983, replaced the concept of special educational treatment with that of 'special educational needs'.

GENERAL DUTIES OF LEAS WITH REGARD TO EDUCATION

Before we consider the particular duties relating to children with special needs, we need to start with the general statutory duty under section 8(1) of the Education Act 1944 relating to education generally. This imposes a general duty on the local education authority to secure that there shall be a sufficient number of schools available for their area:

1. For providing primary education, that is to say, full-time education suitable for the requirements of all junior pupils who have not attained the age of 10 years 6 months, and full-time education suitable to the requirements of junior pupils who have attained that age and whom it is expedient to educate together with junior pupils who have not attained that age (section 8(1)(a)); and

2. For providing secondary education, that is to say, full-time education suitable to the requirements of all pupils of compulsory school age who are either senior pupils, or junior pupils who have attained the age of 10 years 6 months and

whom it is expedient to educate with senior pupils (section 8(1)(b)).

3. Secondary education for those over compulsory school age who still require education at school.

The main duty under section 8 of the 1944 Act is for the local education authority to secure that the schools in the area are sufficient in number, character and equipment to afford for all pupils (as set out under section 8(1) opportunities for education offering such variety and instruction and training as may be desirable in view of their different ages, ability and aptitude, and of the different periods for which they may be expected to remain at school. This includes practical instruction and training appropriate to their respective needs. By section 82 LEAs are required to consider pupils with special educational needs.

The issue of the nature and extent of the statutory duty to provide education was considered by the Court of Appeal in the cases of *E (a Minor) -v- Dorset County Council, Christmas -v- Hampshire County Council, Keating -v- Bromley London Borough Council* 1994 3WLR pg. 853. The plaintiffs in that case claimed for breach of statutory duty not only under the provisions of the Education Act 1944 but also under the provisions of the 1981 Education Act.

The Court of Appeal had cited to it in the Dorset case above, and every case in which Education Acts have been considered since 1908. In two important judgments, which summarised the result of all these cases, Sir Thomas Bingham, the Master of the Rolls, and Lord Justice Evans considered that no action arose for breach of statutory duty giving rise to an individual right for damages, either under the 1944 Education Act section 8, or the provisions of the 1981 Education Act. However, Sir Thomas Bingham stated that, in relation to these duties, he had no doubt that they could be enforced by judicial review (pg. 872 (g)) but they conferred no individual right to damages. Lord Justice Evans, in referring to section 8 of the 1944 Act stated (at pg. 881 (B) to (C)) 'if this duty is not performed, then I have no doubt that it may be enforced by means of legal proceedings commenced on behalf of the child. The correct form of proceedings in the light of the House of Lord's decision in *O'Reilly -v- MacKman 1983* AC pg. 237 is an application for judicial review under R.S.C., Order 53 which is governed by the requirements of the Rules'. The duty to educate can be enforced by judicial review by an individual.

In fulfilling their duties under section 8(2) as amended, the local education authority is required to have regard to:

(i) The need for securing that primary and secondary education is provided in separate schools; and

(ii) The need for securing that special educational provision is made for pupils who have special educational needs. This amendment was introduced by section 2 of the Education Act 1981, section 82(c).

There is therefore a general duty contained in the 1944 Act with a specific requirement to have regard to pupils with special educational needs. The 1981 Education Act, however, introduced more detailed specific obligations on local education authorities to make provision for children with special educational needs. The 1993 Education Act clarified and strengthens those duties.

DEFINITION OF SPECIAL EDUCATIONAL NEEDS AND
SPECIAL EDUCATIONAL PROVISION

If this work were intended to be a legal textbook, the logical place to start would have been with the definition of a child with special educational needs and the legal definition of special educational provision. It does, however, start from the position of a parent, who seeks to identify a child as having special educational needs. This means that either the child will already be the subject of some special educational provision (in the majority of cases) and this issue will not be in dispute or, if no help is being given, the issue is actually the subject of a statement or assessment. In those circumstances legal definitions are better considered in the context of the assessment criteria.

Section 156(1) and (2) of the new Act defines children with special educational needs as those with a learning difficulty. The definition is therefore quite simple. A child has special educational needs if the child has a learning difficulty which calls for special educational provision to be made for him. Section 156(1) to (4) is expressed in exactly the same terms as section 1 of the Education Act 1981. There is no change. The categories of children with learning difficulties described in sub-section 2 are extremely wide and cover all possible disabilities which create for the child a significantly greater difficulty in learning than the majority of children of his age, or a disability which prevents or hinders the child from making use of educational facilities of the kind generally provided for children of his age in schools in the area. Taylor J commented in *R -v- Hampshire Education Authority ex parte J 84 LGR* pg. 547, that not only was this definition extremely wide (p. 566), but it was intended to extend the number of those who fell within this definition of a wider range of difficulties than the 1944 Act covered.

LEARNING DIFFICULTY

The definition of learning difficulty for children with special educational needs is unchanged between section 1 of the Education Act 1981 and section 156(1) of the Education Act 1993.

For the purposes of the Education Act 1993, a child is defined as having special educational needs if he has a learning difficulty which calls for special educational provision to be made for him (section 156(1)).

A child is not to be taken as having a learning difficulty solely because the language or form of language which is or will be taught at school is different from the language or form of language which is at any time being spoken at his home (section 156(3)). Therefore it does not include those who have difficulty with language due to the fact that they do not speak English, either because of their home environment or because they have come from abroad.

The term 'learning difficulty' is defined in the following terms by section 156(2):

1. He has a significantly greater difficulty in learning than the majority of the children of his age;

2. He has a disability which either prevents or hinders him from making use of the educational facilities of the kind generally provided for children of his age in schools in the area of the local education authority; or

3. He is under the age of five years and is or would be if special educational provision were not made for him likely to fall within paragraphs 1. or 2. when over that age.

Thus where a child is under the age of five years, the test is slightly less strict. However, this is a very wide definition and includes all children who have significantly greater difficulty in learning than the majority of children of their age, or any disability which prevents or hinders a child from making use of the educational facilities of the kind provided generally for children of his age in schools in the area of the local authority. It is difficult to imagine a wider definition, and there is no doubt that all the forms of problems which can result in a learning difficulty are plainly encompassed in this definition. In *R -v- Hampshire Education Authority, ex parte J 84 LGR 547*, Taylor J pointed out that this definition was intended to extend and not restrict the definition of children with special educational needs and was wider than the 1944 Act definition. In considering the 1981 Act, which is expressed in exactly the same terms, the Court of Appeal in *R -v- The Secretary of State for Education and Science ex parte E. (1992) 1 FLR* pg. 377 at pg. 388F stated 'the 1981 Act looks at the whole child. A child has special educational needs if he has a learning difficulty which requires special educational provision. Of course a child may have more than one learning difficulty', *per* Balcombe L J. The duty therefore follows, if the child has a learning difficulty which calls for special educational provision to be made for the child.

SPECIAL EDUCATIONAL PROVISION SECTION 156

In the Education Act 1993, Special Educational Provisions means:

1. In relation to a child who has attained the age of two years, educational provision which is additional to, or otherwise different from the Educational Provision made generally for children of his age in schools maintained by the local education authority (other than special schools) or grant-maintained schools in their area; and

2. In relation to a child under that age, educational provision of any kind. For those under two years any educational provision is therefore special educational provision. So far as those who have attained the age of two years, the phrase 'made generally for children of his age' means 'provided to the general run of normal children to the normal majority'. While it has been said that tuition in Greek or music may be additional to the provisions made generally for the majority of children, such tuition cannot be special educational provision because it must be read in conjunction with sub-section 1 which means that the provision is one which is

called for by the learning difficulty, *per Taylor J in R -v- Hampshire Education Authority ex parte J 86 LGR* at pp.547–555, p.556. The provision is therefore something called for by a learning difficulty which is different from that generally provided or available in local schools.

THE DUTY OF LOCAL EDUCATION AUTHORITIES

The local education authority is obliged to keep under review the arrangements made by them for special educational provision in their area. Section 159 of the Act creates this obligation and requires them in so doing to consider the extent to which it is necessary or desirable for the purposes of coordinating provision for children with special educational needs to consult the funding authority (for grant-maintained schools) and governing bodies of council, voluntary, maintained special and grant-maintained schools in their area. So in addition to the general duty on the authority under section 8(2)(c) of the 1944 Act to have regard to the need for providing for children with special educational needs, there is a particular duty to keep under review the arrangements made by the authority for special educational provision and to coordinate those arrangements with all governing bodies in the area together with the funding body for grant-maintained schools.

Section 160 creates a qualified duty to secure education of children with special educational needs in ordinary schools. Any person exercising the functions under Part III of the Act in relation to children with special educational needs should ensure that, if the conditions mentioned in sub-section 2 are satisfied, the child is educated in a school which is not a special school, unless that is incompatible with the wishes of his parent.

Section 160(2) provides that the education of a child with special needs in a school which is not a special school must be compatible with:

1. His receiving the special educational provision which his learning difficulty calls for;

2. The provision of efficient education for the children with whom he will be educated; and

3. The efficient use of resources.

Section 160 is derived from section 2(2) and (3) of the 1981 Act, but with significant modifications. It gives effect to the principle, emphasised in the White Paper 'Choice and Diversity' (Command 2021), that pupils with special educational needs should be educated in an ordinary school to the maximum extent possible. It does this by imposing a duty on any person exercising functions under this part of this Act in respect of a child with special needs who should be educated in a school, to secure that the child is educated in a school which is not a special school. The duty is not confined, as it was under the 1981 Act, to statemented children. The duty must be satisfied by complying with the conditions set out in sub-section (2) which are specified above.

The duty is disapplied if educating the child in this way is incompatible with the wishes of the parents. Although it was suggested in debate in Parliament that this provision gave the parents a right of veto over a placement in an ordinary school, this view is contrary to the Parliament's intention and would seem to be mistaken. The provision merely disapplies the duty under this section, but the LEA retains a discretion, subject to the other provisions of this Act.

The section must be read together with schedule 10 where the LEA was required to specify (section 168) the school for which the parents have expressed a preference, but again they are relieved of this duty, and may insert a different school, if the parents' preferred school is unsuitable to the child's age, ability and aptitude or his special needs, or his attendance at the school would be incompatible with the efficient education of his peers or the efficient use of resources.

In debate, Baroness Blatch, in the House of Lords, stated that the 'crucial considerations determining the LEA's decision are that the placement should be appropriate to the child, appropriate to his peers and compatible with the efficient use of public resources. They cannot allow the parent's views to override these fair and reasonable considerations; "we cannot give the parents a veto".'

This section therefore, although oddly worded, gives effect to the duty to educate in the ordinary school, if compatible with, in particular, the child's special needs, the use of resources and the efficient education of other children.

The LEA must also take into account the provisions of section 76 of the Education Act 1944, which provides for children to be educated in accordance with the wishes of their parents. Although the

LEA must have regard to these wishes, the wishes are not overriding, and are merely one factor in the decision on the child's education *Watt -v- Kesteven County Council 1955 1QB at pg. 408.*

TO WHOM DOES THIS DUTY APPLY?

A child under the 1993 Act includes any person for the purposes of the Act who has not attained the age of 19 years and is a registered pupil at the school. A local education authority cannot therefore divest its statutory responsibilities to young persons who are between 16 and 19 years who fall within this definition.

Where a young person is over compulsory school age, the duty only applies on the basis that they are registered at a school maintained by the local education authority or the Grant-Maintained Funding Council, or are placed at a school under a statement of special educational needs outside of the LEA's sector. Where a young person is over the age of compulsory schooling (16) and is not registered at a local school, then the duty no longer applies, and that young person falls within the area of the Further and Higher Education Funding Council, and its statutory duty under section 4 of the 1992 Education Act, section 165.

THE FULL EXTENT OF THE DUTY PLACED UPON LOCAL EDUCATION AUTHORITIES

The Education Act 1981 created two categories of pupils with special educational needs. These were those for whom a local education authority determined to make a statement of special educational needs in their discretion, and those children whose difficulties could be met by special educational provision determined and provided by the local school (*R -v- Secretary of State for Education and Science, ex parte Lashford* (1988) 1 FLR 72). The introduction of these two categories was a new development, in that the 1944 Act recognised children who required special educational treatment. The Education Act 1993 continues the two different categories, namely, those with a statement of special educational needs who receive special protection, and those for whom the ordinary school is making provision. It is deceptive and confusing to discuss the general duty of local education authorities and schools without bearing in mind this difference in protection. These different categories will be considered in much greater detail in later chapters, but to make sense of the Act one must understand this categorisation.

THE GENERAL DUTY TO ASSESS AND IDENTIFY CHILDREN WITH SPECIAL EDUCATIONAL NEEDS

Section 165 requires that a local education authority shall exercise its powers with a view to securing that of the children for whom it is responsible, they identify those with special educational needs, for whom it is necessary that the authority determine the special educational provision which any learning difficulty he may have calls for (section 165(2)). Therefore, duty is targeted to identify children who will or may require statements of special educational needs. (The meaning of the word 'necessary', which appears in all the statutory provisions concerning assessment and statements, is considered on pp.12–13.)

There is a continuing general duty on the local education authority to make arrangements for children with educational needs created by section 159.

In section 165, the specific duties of the LEA are to identify, and later to assess or make a statement, together with the duty imposed for non-statemented children or schools.

DUTIES OF GOVERNING BODIES OF SCHOOLS IN RELATION TO PUPILS WITH SPECIAL EDUCATIONAL NEEDS

By section 161, the governing bodies of all schools which are in the public sector, whether they be county, voluntarily or grant-maintained schools and in the case of the maintained nursery school, the local education authority itself shall:

1. Use their best endeavours, in exercising their functions in relation to the school, to secure that, if any registered pupils have special educational needs, the special educational provision which his learning difficulty calls for is made for him.

2. Secure that, where the responsible person has been informed by the local education authority that the registered pupil has special educational needs, those needs are made known to all who are likely to teach him; and

3. Secure that the teachers in the school are aware of the importance of identifying and providing for those registered pupils who have special educational needs.

The governing body is also therefore required to use its best endeavours to secure that the special educational provision which a learning difficulty calls for is made for a child with special educational needs. The duty extends not only to identification of the child, but to circumstances where the child has been identified by the local education authority.

The concept of a responsible person in sub-section 1 is defined in sub-section 161(2) as, in the case of a county, voluntarily or grant-maintained school, the head teacher or the appropriate governor (which means the chairman of the governing body or a governor designated for that purpose), and in a nursery school, the head teacher.

THE DUTY OF GOVERNING BODIES TO CONSULT FOR THE PURPOSES OF CO-ORDINATED POLICIES OF SPECIAL EDUCATIONAL PROVISION

In exercising their functions, section 166 obliges governing bodies to consult the local education authority, the funding authority for grant maintained schools and the governing bodies of other schools. The LEA has a similar duty in the case of nursery schools. This is intended to ensure there is a consistent application of provision in the local authority's area. There is a duty on all schools to ensure, so far as is reasonably practical and compatible with the child receiving the special educational provision which he requires, the provision of efficient education for the other children with whom he is educated and the efficient use of resources, that he engages in the activities of the school together with other children who do not have special educational needs.

The major problem with this duty is that, although there is a specific duty in the case of statemented children which is mandatory, the duty on governing bodies *vis-à-vis* non-statemented children is to use their best endeavours to secure provision. It is also required by section 165(5) that in their annual report they must include information about the implementation of the governing body's policy for pupils with special needs. This new provision requires the governing bodies (some of whom will not have considered these issues at all in the past) to address these matters. However, a duty to use best endeavours is not a mandatory duty to make special educational provisions. The parents will be concerned with getting the required provision for the child, not with whether the governing body is using its best endeavours. This duty is assisted by the Code of Practice and section 157.

PROVISION: PRACTICAL ISSUES

Equally, provision made by the Act must be special educational provision, not special provision or merely educational provision. This is an important distinction, because the child may need provision to be educated. For example, a child with a speech difficulty may need speech therapy, which may be either educational or medical; in most cases, it is in fact both. If it is essential to the child's education, it will be a special educational need – see *R -v- Lancaster County Council ex parte CM 1989 2 FLR p.287)*. The Court of Appeal held *in ex parte CM* that speech therapy, which was essential for a child's education, was the special educational provision arising out of the need, although it was normally provided by health authorities. The Court of Appeal held that, if a health authority could not help, then the LEA should go to other health authorities or to the private sector or employ a speech therapist.

A social or religious factor arising out of a child's family background or community could be a special educational need which requires special educational provision. For example, a child from a strictly religious background with a disability, such as Down's syndrome, may not be able to cope in a secular school. Factors such as a diet, religious observance, moral habits and teaching may be significantly different. This will affect the child's ability to learn if the child is puzzled, stressed or unhappy in such circumstances. In *R -v- The Secretary of State for Education and Science ex parte Goldblatt Crown Office Digest 1990 pg. 65*, the Secretary of State for Education conceded and the Court accepted that a religious background giving rise to a need for education in a school of a certain religion was capable of being a need that required provision within the meaning of that Act. This approach was clearly adopted in the previous ministerial circular 22/89. This type of situation is not clearly explained in the present Code of Practice, very probably because the Code of Practice attempts to define in some detail the more common types of disability, and suggest appropriate provision for such disabilities. On a practical rather than a legal basis, learning difficulties are dealt with within the Code of Practice in Chapter 3 paragraphs 46 to 94. It is quite obvious that these are illustrations of particular learning difficulties and are by no means any attempt to define all possible learning difficulties, in particular the rarer types of disability. The Code of Practice provides guidance in general to learning difficulties and special educational provision and in particular to the following categories:

1. Specific learning difficulties: Chapter 3, paragraphs 60 to 63.

2. Emotional and behavioural difficulties: Chapter 3, paragraphs 64 to 70.

3. Physical disabilities: Chapter 3, paragraphs 71 to 74.

4. The sensory impairment: Chapter 5, paragraphs 75 to 80.

5. Sensory impairment visual difficulties: Chapter 3, paragraphs 81 to 84.

6. Speech and language difficulties: Chapter 3, paragraphs 85 to 88.

7. Medical conditions: Chapter 3, paragraphs 89 to 94.

NON-EDUCATIONAL PROVISION

The local education authority has power not only to arrange provision which is educational but also non-educational and medical matters (section 168(5)(a)(ii)). Plainly, if such provision is essential or important to the overall provision for the child, the LEA ought to exercise its discretion in favour of making the provision. It retains a general discretion under this section.

SPECIAL EDUCATIONAL PROVISION OTHERWISE GIVEN IN SCHOOL

By section 163, the local education authority, where it is satisfied that special educational provision is inappropriate, or any part of it can be made in a school for a child with a statement, may arrange the provision otherwise than in a school as part of it. By section 163(2), before making such an arrangement, the local education authority must consult the child's parents.

PROVISION OUTSIDE ENGLAND AND WALES

Section 164(1) requires the local education authority to make such arrangements as they think fit to enable a child for whom they maintain a statement under section 168 of the Act to attend an institution outside England and Wales which specialises in providing for children with special needs. By section 164(2) the definition of children with special needs is extended to cover children who have particular needs which would be special educational needs if those children were in England and Wales.

The duty of the LEA is covered by the regional definition set out in section 165(3). It essentially gives jurisdiction to the LEA in the following categories:

1. Pupils who are registered at maintained, grant-maintained, or grant-maintained special schools.

2. Pupils whose education is provided for them within an independent school specialise or otherwise or by another local authority school at the expense of the LEA or a funding authority.

3. Pupils registered at a school not falling within (1) or (2) above who have been brought to the attention of the authority as having, or probably having, special educational needs; or

4. A pupil who is not registered and not under the age of two years or over 16 but is being brought to their attention as having or probably having special educational needs.

All these categories are limited to children in that area, and children for whom education is provided from the area or out of county by the LEA and are drawn to the authority's attention. All the above categories are based on geography and on the pupil being normally within England and Wales. The effect of section 164 is to make relevant the fact that that child may already be placed at an institution outside England and Wales by his parents or guardian, and brings the child into the LEA's jurisdiction.

Where a local education authority makes arrangements under section 164, those arrangements may include contributing to or paying following:

1. Fees charged by the institution.

2. Expenses reasonably incurred in maintaining the pupil while he is at the institution or travelling to or from it.

3. His travelling expenses; and

4. Expenses reasonably incurred by any person accompanying the pupil while he is travelling or staying at the institution.

This section is without prejudice to any other powers of the local education authority. This power, therefore, enables local education authorities to pay the whole part of the expenses and fees in such a case.

Obviously, where a child requires such a provision, the local authority would perform its duty to make provision for the child, or be under an obligation to make such a placement. However, the local authority is given an extremely wide discretion by this section if matters are not clear cut, and can equally contribute to all relevant expenses or proportion of the expenses and fees incurred.

AGE

Section 156(5) defines a child as any person who has not attained the age of 19 years and is a registered pupil at the school. This responsibility is therefore being adopted by an LEA for a child by way of a statement. The jurisdiction of the Act continues until the age of 19 years or until the child leaves school, whichever is the earlier.

NON-EDUCATIONAL PROVISION AND DISTRICT HEALTH AUTHORITIES

The major problem with the 1981 Education Act was the reluctance of district health authorities. They felt their priorities lay elsewhere than to provide adequate speech therapy or indeed, in some cases, occupational therapy and physiotherapy for children with special educational needs, particularly those who are the subject of a statement. Section 166 provides the means whereby local education authorities can request the help of a district health authority or another local authority by specifying the action in question (section 166(1)).

Section 166(2) requires an authority whose help is requested to comply with that request unless:

1. They consider that the help is not necessary for the purpose of the exercise by the local education authority of those functions; or

2. (i) If the district health authority considers that, with regard to the resources available to them for the purpose of the exercise of their statutory functions under the National Health Service Act 1977, it is not reasonably for them to comply with the request.

   (ii) In the case of a local authority, if they consider that the request is not compatible with their own statutory duty, or other duties or obligations, or unduly prejudices the discharge of their functions.

By section 166(4), regulations may provide that, where an authority is under a duty by virtue of sub-section 2 to comply with a request to help a local education authority in the making of an assessment under section 167 or a statement under section 168 it must, subject to the prescribed exceptions, comply with the request within the prescribed period. This sub-section is therefore intended to impose time limits on district health authorities or other local authorities in the assessment or statementing process.

The most important change in the provisions is that it does now give a local education authority a statutory power to request and impose compulsion on district health authorities in relation to the provision of such services as speech therapy, and in relation to applying with time limits in the process of assessment or compiling a statement.

While these powers are important to local education authorities, parents will be more interested in whether the provision to be made is enough, and so long as the local education authority make sure it is provided, are generally not interested in this type of dispute. As previously considered, the overriding duty to provide any provision which is educational lies on the local education authority, and by statute it must make such arrangements, irrespective of any dispute of the district health authority or any other local education authority.

Chapter 5

The Code of Practice on the Identification and Assessment of Special Educational Needs

The 1981 Education Act was implemented in the light of a series of ministerial circulars. The last and most comprehensive of those circulars was Circular 22/89. Useful though the circulars were, they were hardly a comprehensive guide to the identification and assessment of children with special educational needs. A major change introduced by the 1993 Act was the introduction of a Code of Practice.

Section 157(1) provides that the Secretary of State shall issue, and may from time to time revise, a Code of Practice giving practical guidance in respect of the discharge by local education authorities, the governing bodies of all state schools, the Funding Council for grant maintained schools and any other person exercising functions under Part III of the Act. This means that the guidance applies to all those who work in the state system. All who are dealing with issues concerning children with special needs will, in fact, have to be familiar with it, and use it where relevant.

Sub-Section (2) provides it shall be the duty of

(i) local education authorities, and such governing bodies, exercising functions under this part of this Act, and

(ii) any other person exercising any function for the purpose of the discharge by local education authorities, and such governing bodies, of functions under this part of this Act,

to have regard to the provisions of the code.

Further, the Act provides for a new Appeal Tribunal to have jurisdiction under the Act. Sub-Section (3) gives guidance to the tribunal in the following terms.

(iii) On any appeal, the Tribunal shall have regard to any provision of the code which appears to the Tribunal to be relevant to any question arising on the appeal.

In essence, all concerned with this system must have regard to the Code of Practice or, as the Code itself recognises, some suitable alternative policy.

Section 157 Sub-Section (4) requires the Secretary of State to publish the Code which is in force at that time. Section 158 deals with the making of the Code. The Secretary of State is required to prepare a draft Code or a revised draft Code. Having prepared such a draft the Secretary of State shall consult such persons as he thinks fit and consider any representations made by them. If the Secretary of State determines to proceed with the draft either in its original form or a modified form he shall lay it before both Houses of Parliament. By Section 158(4), if the code is approved it shall come into effect on the day the Secretary of State may by order appoint.

THE STATUS OF THE CODE

What, in fact, do the words 'have regard to' mean in practice? There was some important debate in the House of Lords in Committee and in the Lords, where consideration took place of the amendments on the legal effects of the requirements of the word *have regard to* in relation to the Code. An amendment to change this wording so that the Code would be binding in law eventually failed in Parliament. Clearly, it is not therefore to be applied as a rigid set of legal rules.

In the committee stage in the House of Lords, the Minister of State, Baroness Blatch, explained at some length the Government's thinking in relation to the Code which, together with Act and Regulations would set the framework for special education. She stated that the Code was intended to deal with matters which are not susceptible to hard and fast rules since these are matters where an element of judgment is always required. Further, the code reaches much wider than merely giving guidance to simply the education authority or, in fact, the special needs tribunal. It has a bearing on health services and social service function. No doubt these were considerations which led the government to defeat the amendment to make the Code legally binding.

The Code was intended and is intended to promote a consistent approach to special education across England and Wales. Equally, is it intended to deal both with those who will need a statement and those who will not need a statement; the majority of children with special educational needs.

However, an important debate took place on the Code in the House of Lords when Baroness Blatch clarified the Government's thinking on these issues (Hansard Vol. 554 No. 83, paragraphs 14.13 and 14.17). Baroness Blatch stated 'as the Foreword (to the Code) explains, the effect of having regard to the Code may vary according to the circumstances and over time. Clearly one cannot expect all schools and LEAs to have undertaken a comprehensive study of the Code and to have changed their procedures accordingly in September 1994. But it is reasonable to expect them to have regard to the Code from that point and to plan future action in the light of the Code.

The Independent Special Needs Tribunal will also be under a duty to have regard to the Code of Practice. This will serve as an added incentive to LEAs to have regard to the Code. The Tribunal will not exercise a general oversight of LEAs' adherence to the Code's provisions. The Tribunal's task will be to consider appeals in cases where parents have exercised their right of appeal under the 1993 Act.' The statement in the draft Foreword to the code was quoted by Baroness Blatch 'the Tribunal will expect LEAs to be able to justify any departure from the Code where such a departure was relevant to the decision in question'. However, an LEA could ignore the code and be right. If it is ignored, or not applied, they will no doubt have to justify their actions.

Baroness Blatch made it clear that the impact of the Code depended upon the effectiveness of the procedures which were put in place.

Everybody working in this field must have a copy of the Code. It is a very long document which will not be described in detail and this chapter considers some general issues which will relate to appeals. The essential feature of the Code is that it is a three-stage school-based procedure of assessment and provision; at stage 4 a statutory assessment takes place and stage 5 is the statemented child (Stages 4 and 5 are considered in more detail in Chapters 7 and 8, in their context) . The Code recognises that efficient variations can be adopted. For example, some LEAs have adopted a two-stage school-based assessment procedure, yet the Code adopts a three-stage version.

The greatest defect of the Code, which is a good document, is that it is silent on the issue of what happens if a child has special needs, and one would expect the child's needs to be catered for at the lower level under the Code, but that help is simply not there as the school or the local education authority has not the resources available, or these are not made available. Plainly, on the facts, one may consider it is necessary to make a statement in those circumstances, because the LEA would not implement the provisions of the Code, and the help is not there. This important problem is avoided. Equally, the Code expects the ordinary school to have experience in many areas of disability, yet this may not be the case.

The Code contains a great deal of statements of good intention, rather than guidance, or firm practice.

The Tribunal most certainly will seek to have regard to the Code but as appropriate to the factual situation, this might result in a statement or an assessment of the child's special educational needs depending upon the circumstances. A local education authority which does not implement the Code or is not able to put the Code into place initially or for some time, can therefore expect the Tribunal to have regard to failure to apply the Code, and order action to be taken, where the correct facilities are not available. Yet the Tribunal may perfectly properly consider, in a neighbouring county, that adequate provision is being made and the Code was not implemented in so far as the issue before it is concerned. However, the Code is not a rigid straightjacket and cases should not normally depend on a rigid checklist of the code. The Code can be ignored, and yet the LEA could be absolutely right.

The statutory provisions fall far short of making the code mandatory. This of course is a perfectly sensible approach to matters, as at the time the 1993 Act Part 3 was passed there were no accepted national standards, and procedures varied from county to county. Some areas will have provision which is regarded as very good and detailed assessment procedures, but others simply do not have the same facilities. In the long run, it is plainly the government's intention, the intention of the Act, and the hope of all concerned, that the Code of Practice and the statutory provisions will give rise to an increasing awareness of the requirements for dealing with children with special needs as early as possible and identifying their special educational needs in an efficient and appropriate manner.

The fundamental principles of the Code are set out in the introductory section and are as follows:

- the needs of all pupils who may have special educational needs either throughout, or at any time during, their school careers must be addressed; the Code recognises that there is a continuum of needs and a continuum of provision, which may be made in a wide variety of different forms
- children with special educational needs require the greatest possible access to a broad and balanced education, including the National Curriculum
- the needs of most pupils will be met in the mainstream, and without a statutory assessment or statement of special educational needs. Children with special educational needs, including children with statements of special educational needs, should, where appropriate and taking into account the wishes of their parents, be educated alongside their peers in mainstream schools
- even before he or she reaches compulsory school age a child may have special educational needs requiring the intervention of the LEA as well as the health services
- the knowledge, views and experience of parents are vital. Effective assessment and provision will be secured where there is the greatest possible degree of partnership between parents and their children and schools, LEAs and other agencies.

The practices and procedures essential in pursuit of these principles are that:

- all children with special educational needs should be identified and assessed as early as possible and as quickly as is consistent with thoroughness
- provision for all children with special educational needs should be made by the most appropriate agency. In most cases this will be the child's mainstream school, working in partnership with the child's parents: no statutory assessment will be necessary

- where needed, LEAs must make assessments and statements in accordance with the prescribed time limits; must write clear and thorough statements, setting out the child's educational and non-educational needs, the objectives to be secured, the provision to be made and the arrangements for monitoring and review; and ensure the annual review of the special educational provision arranged for the child and the updating and monitoring of educational targets
- special educational provision will be most effective when those responsible take into account the ascertainable wishes of the child concerned, considered in the light of his or her age and understanding
- there must be close co-operation between all the agencies concerned and a multi-disciplinary approach to the resolution of issues.

The guidance in the Code is drafted subject to the matters set out above and must be borne clear in mind. The first three stages are based in the school, which will as necessary call upon the help of external specialists. At Stages 4 and 5 the LEA are expected by the Code to share the responsibility with schools. Stages 4 and 5 are basically the assessment stages and, if a statement is necessary, the statement stage. The stages are described in the Code as follows:

Stage 1: class or subject teachers identify or register a child's special educational needs and, consulting the school's SEN co-ordinator, take initial action (The SEN co-ordinator is the member of the school's staff who is responsible for SEN in the school.)

Stage 2: the school's SEN co-ordinator takes lead responsibility for gathering information and for co-ordinating the child's special educational provision, working with the child's teachers

Stage 3: teachers and the SEN co-ordinator are supported by specialists from outside the school

Stage 4: the LEA consider the need for a statutory assessment and, if appropriate, make a multidisciplinary assessment

Stage 5: the LEA consider the need for a statement of special
educational needs and, if appropriate, make a
statement and arrange, monitor and review provision.

As the tribunal will have regard to any provision of the Code which
appears to the tribunal to be relevant to any question arising on
appeal, the principles adopted by the Code are an important development. The principles are designed to be action in partnership with
parents to secure appropriate provision for children with special
needs and to minimise disputes, thereby avoiding appeals. The
overriding interests of the Code and all concerned is to make sure
that provision is made for the child with special educational needs.

IS THE RIGID APPLICATION OF THE CODE NECESSARY IN ALL CASES?

The Code clearly directs the attention of all concerned to the fact that
many children will need to move into the system more quickly. This
should be remembered by all. It is, however, weak on the need for
an assessment irrespective of whether the school-based stages 1 to
3 have been completed, where such a need exists.

Section 173 provides for a parent to request an assessment of their
child's needs, where a statement is not maintained under section
168, or if such an assessment has not been made within the period
of six months ending with the date on which the request is made. By
section 173(1)(c), an assessment should be made if it is necessary for
the authority to make such an assessment, and the authority shall
comply with that request. The parent has a right of appeal in the
event of the request being refused.

Equally, the governing body of a grant-maintained school is given
the right to make such a request in respect of the child who is placed
at the school under a direction made by section 13 of the Act. The
test for assessment is the same, namely, is it necessary. Neither the
Act nor the Code contemplates that in appropriate cases children
who require over and above that which is normally available in the
ordinary school from its special needs expertise will have to wait to
go through a set procedure as outlined in the Code. The Code
recognises that there are children who need an immediate referral
for statutory assessment; however, the examples given are somewhat limited as the Code has confined itself to the more obvious and

severe problems – in Chapter 3 paragraphs 3.24 to 3.26. These are only examples, and are not an exhaustive list.

In relation to the criteria for making an assessment in such circumstances, detailed guidance is given by the Code, and it is likely that the tribunal will order an assessment in the following circumstances:

1. Where the disability is obviously a ·disability that needs extra help and resources which are not normally available in an ordinary school.

2. Even if the school is of the view it can cope, if the parents can show the school has not adequately coped and/or does not adequately understand the child's needs and problems, so that intervention is necessary.

3. Where there is an obvious need for immediate action such as emotional problems developing into a severe difficulty, development of medical problems or psychiatric problems, where the child refuses to attend school as the child has become school phobic, or where the needs are misunderstood or undetected and the child is far behind.

These illustrations are not, of course, exhaustive. An important consideration will obviously be where, on the facts, in the light of the child's special educational needs and requirements for provision, it is obvious that the school itself has not available adequate expertise provision. At the beginning of this new statutory system it is likely that this consideration will play an important part in some decisions made.

It is most important for parents to remember that if they are contemplating bypassing the early assessment procedures in the Code they will have to justify their case clearly. It should be borne in mind that in the cases of most children, it is only after the school's resources, with some extra help from the authority, has been tried that it can be seen that the child plainly needs greater and extra help. Equally, there will be cases where it is obvious that the child's learning difficulties are sufficiently severe to justify moving forward more quickly to the statement process.

SCHOOL-BASED STAGES OF ASSESSMENT AND PROVISION

The provisions of the Code in relation to statements, and assessments are considered separately in context. The Code in the five stages of assessment adopts generally the stages used by the Warnock report. However, the Code in Chapter 2, paragraph 2 at long last sounds a note of caution in relation to the Warnock committee's estimate of the number of children with special needs. The Warnock committee made a 'guestimate' that 20 per cent of children may at some time when they are at school have special educational needs. Of those children it was reckoned that about 2 per cent nationally would require a statement, a small minority of such cases.

These figures were reiterated in the ministerial circulars, and in some local authorities appeared to be applied as some form of undefined rigid criteria. The 1981 Education Act and the 1993 Education Act do not look at percentages of children. Both the 1981 Act and the 1993 Act together with the Code of Practice are looking at the child's needs and requirement for provision on an individual basis. They are not therefore dealing with percentages. The idea of the 2 per cent being treated as a carefully researched, relevant figure to be applied nationally has caused great concern; it was never intended that this be applied as some form of rigid rule.

It is probable from statistics available for some counties, and local authorities, that the actual number of children who should be statemented was always greater than 2 per cent. Whether that be so or not, the Code makes it clear that this is a broad national estimate, and the proportion of children with special needs will vary significantly from area to area. Indeed, it is also probable that clusters of children with particular forms of problems will be found frequently in some area and not in other areas. The Code at long last gives a considerable warning against these figures; however, it is to be regretted the figures of 2 per cent and 20 per cent are repeated by some local authorities, as this can still lead to misunderstandings. It is to be welcomed that the Code clarifies the point.

Also, the Code is obviously drafted on the basis of the respective responsibilities of the governing body section 161, and the local education authority. In particular the governing body must carry out the following tasks:

- do their best to secure that the necessary provision is made for any pupil who has special educational needs
- secure that, where the 'responsible person' – the head teacher or the appropriate governor – has been informed by the LEA that a pupil has special educational needs, those needs are made known to all who are likely to teach him or her
- secure that teachers in the school are aware of the importance of identifying, and providing for, those pupils who have special educational needs
- consult the LEA; as appropriate, the Funding Authority (see Glossary); and the governing bodies of other schools, when it seems to them necessary or desirable in the interests of co-ordinated special educational provision in the area as a whole
- report annually to parents on the school's policy for pupils with special educational needs
- ensure that the pupil joins in the activities of the school together with pupils who do not have special educational needs, so far as that is reasonably practical and compatible with the pupil receiving the necessary special educational provision, the efficient education of other children in the school and the efficient use of resources.

(section 161)

- have regard to this Code of Practice when carrying out their duties toward all pupils with special educational needs.

(section 157)

It is the responsibility of the governing body to decide how best to provide for children with special educational needs. The Code of Practice recommends that the governing body delegate their responsibility to an individual member of the body, the head teacher or the co-ordinator of the special educational needs (SEN) team. The Code expects, however, that arrangements are made for the governing body closely to monitor the work of the school on behalf of pupils with special educational needs. The Act reinforces the duty on the governing body by requiring by regulation prescribed issues to be addressed in the school's policies which include:

1. Basic information about the school's special educational provision:

   - the objectives of the school's SEN policy
   - the name of the school's SEN co-ordinator or teacher responsible for the day-to-day operation of the SEN policy
   - the arrangements for co-ordinating educational provision for pupils with SEN
   - admission arrangements
   - any SEN specialism and any special units
   - any special facilities which increase or assist access to the school by pupils with SEN.

2. Information about the school's policies for identification, assessment and provision for all pupils with SEN:

   - the allocation of resources to and amongst pupils with SEN
   - identification and assessment arrangements; and review procedures
   - arrangements for providing access for pupils with SEN to a balanced and broadly based curriculum, including the National Curriculum
   - how children with special educational needs are integrated within the school as a whole
   - criteria for evaluating the success of the school's SEN policy
   - arrangements for considering complaints about special educational provision within the school.

3. Information about the school's staffing policies and partnership with bodies beyond the schools:

   - the school's arrangements for SEN in-service training
   - use made of teachers and facilities from outside the school, including support services
   - arrangements for partnership with parents
   - links with other mainstream schools and special schools, including arrangements when pupils change schools or leave school

- links with health and social services, educational welfare services and any voluntary organisations.

Education (Special Educational Needs) (Information) Regulations, regulation 2 and Schedule 1

The Code expects there to be an SEN co-ordinator responsible for the day-to-day operation of the school's SEN policy, advising class and subject teachers, taking the lead in managing provision for pupils, particular at stages 2 and 3, updating and allowing for the keeping records of all pupils with special educational needs, working with the parents of the children, and liaising with external agencies. It is doubtful, in fact, whether before the 1993 Act, these tasks were adequately addressed nationally in some schools. The Code certainly requires a substantial change in practice in many areas by schools.

Chapter 2, paragraph 2.16 of the Code emphasises the importance of early identification assessment and provision for any child who may have special educational needs. The earlier the action is taken, the more responsive the child is likely to be, the more likely it is that the child will be successfully helped without undue intervention. Equally, the Code fully appreciates that if there is an early start, it is more likely that intervention will be successful within the ordinary school.

Chapter 2 of the Code emphasises the importance of record keeping, when working within the school-based assessment stages. Equally, the need to work with and use the expertise of the health services and the local authority social services is made clear and particularly the need for partnership with parents. The Code accepts that the relationship between parents and the school has a crucial bearing on the child's educational progress and on the effectiveness of any school-based intervention. The Code expects the attitude of the school to be a working partnership with the parents and that this will be a practical and effective scheme. The school's arrangements for parents of children with special needs, Chapter 2.33 onwards of the Code of Practice should include the following:

Information

- on the school's SEN policy
- on the support available for children with special educational needs within the school and LEA

- on parents' involvement in assessment and decision-making, emphasising the importance of their contribution
- on services such as those provided by the local authority for children 'in need'
- on local and national voluntary organisations which might provide information, advice or counselling.

Partnership

- arrangements for recording and acting upon parental concerns
- procedures for involving parents when a concern is first expressed within the school
- arrangements for incorporating parents' views in assessment and subsequent reviews.

Access for parents

- information in a range of community languages
- information on tape for parents who may have literacy or communication difficulties
- a parents' room or other arrangements in the school to help parents feel confident and comfortable.

THE INVOLVEMENT OF THE CHILD

The Code equally recognises that the effectiveness of any assessment and intervention will be mainly influenced by the involvement and interests of the child and young persons concerned. Equally the Code accepts in Chapter 2 paragraph 2.34 to 36 that the child or young person has important and relevant information. Further, that children have a right to be heard and should be encouraged to participate in the decision making about provision to meet their needs. The school should make every effort to identify the assessable views and wishes of the child and young person about his or her current education. The Code invites all to consider how they:

1. Involve pupils in the decision making processes.

2. Determine the child's level of participation, bearing in mind the age, ability and past experiences of the child.

3. Record the pupil's views in identifying their difficulties, setting goals, agreeing a development strategy and monitoring and reviewing progress.

4. Involving pupils and implementing individual educational plans.

In appropriate places, where the difficulties seen at school exhibit medical conditions (whether related to the educational needs or whether the disability itself involves a medical condition or one has developed), the child health services are required to be involved. In particular, where the case gives rise to cause for concern, to the general practitioner, health visitor, school health service, or the community paediatrician, whichever is the appropriate expert, the relevant advisory teacher should be consulted. If parents make an expression of anxiety about an aspect of development they should be involved and the relevant professionals consulted. Where such advice is necessary, useful and relevant, the SEN co-ordinator should ensure its confidentiality and keep an effective systems operated by the school for:

1. Keeping any medical records of children with SEN.

2. Drawing together any information available from the general practitioner, school health service, health visitor, community paediatrician, child and adolescent mental health service, or hospital children's department.

3. The transfer of relevant medical information between phases for ensuring thorough co-operation with the relevant professionals, and the elimination of *medical causes* as a possible explanation for observable learning and behavioural difficulties.

4. Identifying early signs of depression and abnormal eating behaviour and substance misuse.

SOCIAL SERVICES AND EDUCATION WELFARE SERVICE

Schools should be aware of the range of social services provided by the education welfare service and the social services department to support children regarded as being in need. They should also be aware of the Social Services Department duty under section 17 of the Children Acts 1989:

(1) It shall be the general duty of every local authority (in addition to the other duties imposed on them by this Part) –

   (a) to safeguard and promote the welfare of children within their area who are in need; and

   (b) so far as is consistent with that duty, to promote the upbringing of such children by their families,

by providing a range and level of services appropriate to those children's needs.

(2) For the purpose principally of facilitating the discharge of their general duty under this section, every local authority shall have the specific duties and powers set out in Part 1 of Schedule 2.

(3) Any service provided by an authority in the exercise of functions conferred on them by this section may be provided for the family of a particular child in need or for any member of his family, if it is provided with a view to safeguarding or promoting the child's welfare.

(4) The Secretary of State may by order amend any provision of Part 1 of Schedule 2 or add any further duty or power to those for the time being mentioned there.

(5) Every local authority –

   (a) shall facilitate the provision by others (including in particular voluntary organisations) of services which the authority have power to provide by virtue of this section, or section 18, 20, 23 or 24; and

   (b) may make such arrangements as they see fit for any person to act on their behalf in the provision of any such service.

(6) The services provided by a local authority in the exercise of functions conferred on them by this section may include giving assistance in kind or, in exceptional circumstances, in cash.

(7) Assistance may be unconditional or subject to conditions as to the repayment of the assistance or of its value (in whole or in part).

(8) Before giving any assistance or imposing any conditions, a local authority shall have regard to the means of the child concerned and of each of his parents.

(9) No person shall be liable to make any repayment of assistance or of its value at any time when he is in receipt of income support or family credit under the Social Security Act 1986.

(10) For the purposes of this Part a child shall be taken to be in need if –

> (a) he is unlikely to achieve or maintain, or to have the opportunity of achieving or maintaining, a reasonable standard of health or development without the provision for him of services by a local authority under this Part;

> (b) his health or development is likely to be significantly impaired, or further impaired, without the provision for him of such services; or

> (c) he is disabled,

and 'family', in relation to such a child, includes any person who has parental responsibility for the child and any other person with whom he has been living.

(11) For the purposes of this Part, a child is disabled if he is blind, deaf or dumb or suffers from mental disorder of any kind or is substantially and permanently handicapped by illness, injury or congenital deformity or such other disability as may be prescribed; and in this Part –

> 'development' means physical, intellectual, emotional, social or behavioural development; and

> 'health' means physical or mental health.

The Code asks the school to provide an integrated approach to the education, health and welfare needs of children with special educational needs. It also requires schools to co-operate with the social services department where it is considered that the child is at risk of abuse or neglect.

A social services department should designate an officer or officers who are responsible for working with schools (Chapter 2, paragraph 2.54). This officer should be available so that schools and the LEA can refer cases for advice. Schools are required to have suitable arrangements for:

1. Liaison with social services.

2. Registering concern about a child's welfare.

3. Putting into practice any local procedures relating to child protection issues.

4. Liaison with the local authority when a child is accommodated by that authority.

5. Obtaining information on services provided by the local authority for children in need.

The 1981 Act was under used for children with learning difficulties, when the Children Act assessment processes were used. Equally, the Children Act assessment processes apply to children with learning difficulties, even if they come from a supporting parental background. The powers under section 17, section 43, and schedule 2 of the Children Act were often ignored, and where a child had a multiplicity of problems and needs, but supportive parents, the Children Act was not used. The Code of Practice directs attention to the necessity for looking at a child in the light of these statutory duties. It remains to be seen whether the Code's overall effect is to make local authorities, whether social services departments or education departments, make more use of these powers in appropriate cases.

SUMMARY OF SCHOOL-BASED STAGES OF ASSESSMENT

The school-based stages should be seen as a continuous and systematic cycle of planning and intervention. There should be the necessary reviews within the school to check progress. It is intended to enable the child with special educational needs to learn and make progress. As Baroness Blatch made clear in the Lord's debate, it is unlikely at the present moment that all schools will be able to apply such a sophisticated and careful system of assessment in a uniform manner in accordance with national accepted standards. It is obviously the intention of the Code that, as time goes on, standards should improve, particularly as schools become more familiar with the system and its requirements.

Stage 1

This envisages class or subject teachers consulting the SEN co-ordinator and identifying the child's special educational needs, assembling information and putting into place any special arrangements to meet those needs and informing the head teacher.

Stage 2

The SEN co-ordinator now takes the lead responsibility for managing the child's special educational provision, working with the child's teachers to devise a more comprehensive set of strategies, and informing the head teacher.

Stage 3

The SEN co-ordinator continues to lead responsibility and should always consult and inform the head teacher. Specialist staff from outside the school, such as the educational psychologist, and advisory teachers with special qualifications, are brought in to help the school support a child with more complex needs. Should the child still not progress satisfactorily, a specialist will help the school consider whether the child is likely to meet the criteria for statutory assessment.

At the end of each stage, the Code indicates that the progress of the child should be reviewed, following each stage of planned intervention. The Code requires progress to be review. The class teacher and the SEN co-ordinator will decide whether they are applying each stage to:

1. Continue the child's current educational arrangements

2. seek further advice; or

3. draw up a plan using the expertise within the school, initially, and at the end of each stage;

4. review the progress made by the child;

5. the effectiveness of the education plan;

6. the updated information and advice available in the light of the child's progress or lack of progress; and

7. decide on future action.

At each stage the decision will involve either a decision that no further help is needed, or that the child remains at the same stage, or that the child should move forward into the next stage.

Each stage requires an education plan for the child, as well as to review any decision making process. Stage 2, the more sophisticated stage, involves consideration of non-curriculum issues such as the pastoral care arrangements, medical requirements and the like.

Stage 3

Obviously stage 3 is the stage which can be regarded in normal cases as the threshold to a statement. If intervention is effective, then it is a success. If Stage 3 does not work, one would expect certainly an assessment, and very possibly a statement. However, stage 3 is not simply a stage that should be used following stages 1 and 2.

The Code makes it clear that in some cases children will need early intensive intervention, but not necessarily an assessment or statement. In the cases of such children the SEN co-ordinator, teachers and parents should discuss the issues, and the SEN co-ordinator, having consulted the head teacher, can put into place early intensive intervention and bring in external support where it is immediately necessary.

Such support will come from teachers in learning or behaviour support services, peripatetic teachers, the educational psychologists, child health or mental health services, social services and advisors or teachers with knowledge or information of technology. Equally, where help is available from special public publications or specialist help from organisations who deal with particular problems of the disabled, such as the National Council for Educational Technology, this should be sought. The SEN co-ordinator is expected by the Code to be familiar with the relevant information and local practices.

Stage 3 is therefore also an alternative form of assessment on a less sophisticated basis to the assessment procedures envisaged by statute and regulation. The SEN co-ordinator will review the position, assuming the child has gone through Stages 1 and 2. This will include information gathered at that point and the report compiled at the end of review stage 2.

Equally, stage 3 should lead to consideration as to whether an assessment is necessary at this stage and the decision made should include consideration of whether further advice is necessary, the drawing up of a new education plan, including the involvement of the support services. The Code at this stage requires a much more detailed individual education plan which is reproduced below:

Stage 3 – Individual Education Plan

- nature of the child's learning difficulty
- action – the special educational provision
  - school staff involved, including frequency and timing of support
  - external specialists involved, including frequency and timing
  - specific programmes/activities/materials/equipment
- help from parents at home
- targets to be achieved in a given time
- any pastoral care or medical requirements
- monitoring and assessment arrangements
- review arrangements and date.

It is important that a review date be set, which may be within half a term but should always be within a term. The SEN co-ordinator should agree with the pupil's teachers and the external specialists who are involved in arrangements about the means of monitoring the child's progress against the objectives which are established in the plan. The SEN co-ordinator should convene a review meeting at the end of the review period and it should focus on:

1. Progress made by the child.

2. Effectiveness of the education plan.

3. Whether a child is likely in the future to be referred for statutory assessment, an important part of the decision-making process.

4. Updated information and advice.

5. Future action.

Obviously, the outcome of the review can be a continuation at stage 3 if progress is satisfactory or non-proven, a reversion to stage 2 if progress is at least satisfactory, or at this stage the head teacher should consider referring the child to the LEA for a statutory assessment if progress is not satisfactory. The Code expects the head teacher to work together with the SEN co-ordinator on this issue.

The Code expects the following information to be available should there be a reference for a statutory assessment:

- information, including:
  - the recorded views of parents and, where appropriate, children on the earlier stages of assessment and any action and support to date
  - evidence of health checks, for example relevant information on medical advice to the school
  - when appropriate, evidence relating to social services involvement
- written individual education plans at stages 2 and 3 indicating the approaches adopted, the monitoring arrangements followed and the educational outcomes
- reviews of each individual education plan indicating decisions made as a result
- evidence of the involvement and views of professionals with relevant specialist knowledge and expertise outside the normal competence of the school.

If the school does not keep the required documentation some LEA officers believe this is a reason to refuse an assessment. Equally, the school may not strictly apply the Code. However, if a parent appeals, the real issue will be the child, and education, not whether the school has applied the Code.

The Code also requires a head teacher to have regard to consider disapplying exemptions to certain parts of the national curriculum under section 19 of the Education Reform Act and give directions modifying the national curriculum. Although this is contained in the Code it is doubted whether this particular provision has any great practical effect. These exemption provisions appeared to be a possible important route to assist children with special needs when the Education Reform Act 1988 was passed. However, in fact they have not been used very frequently, and appear to have been mostly ignored in practice. It is difficult to see that the Code of Practice will result in any large revival of the usage of these powers. It is more likely that the Code, in concentrating on the child, will direct the school's attention to the basic issue which is whether stage 3 has worked sufficiently well to at least continue with it or to take the view that the child is being adequately helped, or whether an assessment is necessary.

Stages 4 and 5 are the statutory assessment and the decision to make a statement. These stages are considered in the light of the statutory provisions in more detail. They also arise in considering the types of appeal. The evidence likely to be required in relation to each appeal is considered. The remainder of the Code is considered in the context of assessments, reviews, statements and appeals in the context of the issues, and the law.

Chapter 6

Children Under the Age of Five Years

Chapter 5 of the Code of Practice deals with children under the age of five years. Section 175 deals with assessments for children under the age of two. By section 175(1), if the authority are of the opinion that a child under the age of two has special educational needs and it is necessary to determine the special educational provision (sub-section 2), then they may, with the consent of the parents, or at the request of his parents, make an assessment of the child's needs. If the LEA form the view that an assessment is necessary, they need parental consent. Obviously, they will in practice not need such consent if the parent makes the request. In this chapter the law and the Code are jointly considered. I will not return to this subject, when considering assessments, and appeals.

Section 175 reflects the old law in this way: the assessment is made in such a manner for young children of this nature as the authority consider appropriate. The statement may be maintained in such a manner as considered appropriate. Bearing in mind these provisions are dealing with help for the more severely disabled child, it is entirely appropriate to have such generalised provisions so that some specific help can be given by way of early intervention.

For children under five, where they are in a maintained nursery, the provisions of section 161 requires the LEA to use its best endeavours to see that provision is made for registered pupils with learning difficulty. However, for children under the age of five attending a maintained nursery school class, the Code states that the LEA may normally expect that a school-based assessment process will be used. However, the Code of Practice seems to be somewhat optimistic in this view as the Code of Practice is really designed to deal with children who are in an ordinary school after the age of five. However, many children attending will be attending pre-school education with provision made by social services, health authorities or from a voluntary or independent charitable sector, because there is a concern about the child or there are identifiable disabilities. In the more obvious cases of disability or problems which have emerged from birth or as a result or accident after birth, assessment should take place. The Code of Practice in paragraph 5(16) provides useful guidance which cannot be improved upon in relation to setting out the criteria for such an assessment.

> 5:16. When a child under five is already attending a maintained nursery school or class the LEA may expect that the broad principles of the school-based stages of assessment, action and review, adapted as appropriate in the light of the circumstances of the school concerned, will be followed as for older children. However, many young children will be attending provision made by social services, the health services or the voluntary or independent sectors when concern about a possible special educational need is first raised. Because early identification should lead to a more timely assessment and intervention which in turn should avoid the escalation of a difficulty into a significant special educational need, it is important that any concern about a child's development and progress should be shared at the earliest possible moment.

The Code of Practice points out that where children between the ages of two and five have complex needs, statutory procedures may be essential in order to maximise their opportunities. It also makes the obvious point that contributions from non-educational services such as medical or social services are likely at this stage to be of key importance. The relevant part of Chapter 5, paragraphs 20 to 24 give good guidance on these issues:

> 5:20. Where children between two and five have such complex needs that statutory procedures may be essential in order to maximise their opportunities, the statement will follow the same format as for any other children. The contributions of non-educational service providers are likely to be of key importance.

> 5:21. LEAs should note that parents of children under five may express a preference for a maintained school to be named in their child's statement and may make representations in favour of a non-maintained or independent school for their child. The LEA

should ensure that parents have full information on the range of provision available within the authority and may wish to offer parents the opportunity to visit such provision and discuss any aspect of the provision with the Named Officer within the LEA. LEAs must provide parents with lists of independent schools approved under section 189 of the Act; all non-maintained special schools; and of all LEA-maintained and grant-maintained schools in the area of the LEA which cater for children of the appropriate age. They may also inform parents of such schools in neighbouring areas.

5:22. LEAs should informally review a statement for a child under five at least every six months to ensure that the provision is appropriate to the child's needs. Such reviews would complement the statutory duty to carry out an annual review in accordance with the Regulations but would not require the same range of documentation so long as they reflected the significant changes which can take place in the progress of a child under the age of five.

Special educational provision for children under five

5:23. For very young children, access to a home-based learning programme or the services of a peripatetic teacher for the hearing or visually impaired may provide the most appropriate help. In the case of a child with a behavioural difficulty, the advice of the clinical psychologist at a child development centre or an educational psychologist may enable the child to remain within an existing service. In some instances there may be a decision that a child should attend a nursery class or school (either within a mainstream or special school setting), playgroup or opportunity playgroup.

5:24. All services working within a local authority with young children, including home-based learning programmes, should have clearly articulated arrangements for access to their services. Those arrangements should be readily understandable by parents of children with special needs; indicate the kind of support which can be provided; and state any priority admission arrangements for such children.

ASSESSMENT AND STATEMENTS FOR CHILDREN UNDER FIVE

Section 175 provides for a statement for children under five if the child has special educational needs and it is necessary for the authority to determine the special educational provision. However, where an assessment of a child under five is contemplated, it is obvious that the child will have a severe problem. It may be that the child is born and diagnosed after birth as disabled or handicapped or it may be apparent that there are obvious disabilities such as those that would include hearing and speech problems.

In such cases, either the parents or the child's health services or social services or all three will have identified the child as having special needs. Children are normally assessed in such cases where it is important to provide help as early as possible.

A decision to make a statement will usually either be because the child has complex needs, or to allow access to a particular service. This could be a home-based teaching service or a developmental play programme. The 1981 Act, and section 175 both allow the local education authority to assess a child in such manner as it considers appropriate. The detailed requirements of the regulations for older children do not apply to such assessments.

However, the Code of Practice stresses a number of factors. LEAs should explain to parents of children under five with special needs their rights in relation to requesting a statutory assessment and the implications of a statement. The parental perspective is particularly important for such children. Such children should be assessed in a place where the child and the family feel comfortable. Access to other parents, family centres, local services, play and opportunity groups are important in such cases and will have a direct impact on these cases.

Where a child is in the nursery class or school, they are expected to follow broadly the same procedure for identifying and meeting the special needs of children under five as in the cases of older children of compulsory school age. If the education/developmental progress of the child under five gives rise to concern, the child's teacher, if the child is at school, should prepare a written report setting out the child's strengths and weaknesses and noting the evidence for concern.

Section 176 provides that district health authorities and national health service trusts must inform the parents and the appropriate LEA when they form the opinion that a child under the age of five may have special educational needs. They must also inform the parents if they believe a particular voluntary organisation is likely to be able to give the parents advice or assistance in connection with any special educational needs that the child may have.

It is likely that this method of notification will be by far the most frequent and indeed the most important. With such children, contact with the child health services is obviously going to be important, so that proper medical advice and professional advice is received to deal with the child's disabilities and behaviour. Where the health authority or trust consider that the child does have special needs, they must inform the parent of their views and give the parents the opportunity to discuss those views with an officer of the health authority or of the trust. Only after this takes place must the LEA then be informed. Health authorities and trusts must give parents the name of voluntary organisation which might be of assistance, if they consider that a child under five may have special needs. The health services should give parents information on the full range of local statutory and voluntary services. For children under five, statements will be rare. The Code of Practice very wisely directs LEAs to first consider programmes of support according to the child's particular needs. There is no statutory framework for this area, and the Code of Practice in paragraph 5.5 indicates that where parents actually request an assessment this indicates that the support is inadequate.

The Code of Practice divides the area of children under the age of five into children under two (paragraph 5.5 to paragraph 5.8) and up to five (paragraph 5.16 to 5.18 inclusive). One would expect there to be more information available on a child attending a nursery school, or a nursery class and where it is likely to be more available. The Code of Practice expects LEAs to adopt similar (but adapted) procedures for these younger children to that used for older children. In reality, however, as these children will have severe problems, what is needed is the appropriate practical approach.

In any event, many young children will be attending provision made by social services, health services or voluntary independent sectors within this category. Intervention will lead to a more timely assessment and provision, which will prevent escalation of the difficulties or, indeed, in some cases eliminate them as the child enters school. It is therefore important that adequate attention is paid to concerns about the child's development.

CRITERIA FOR STATUTORY ASSESSMENTS

1. Where the child is at school what difficulties have been identified by the school?

2. Has the nursery class or school developed full broad-based strategies to assist the child?

3. Where the child is attending health services, social services, voluntary or private provision, have any concerns been raised about his or her development, has any outside advice been sought regarding the child's:

    (i) physical health and function;

    (ii) communication skills;

    (iii) perceptual and motor skills;

    (iv) self-help skills;

    (v) social skills;

    (vi) emotional and behavioural development; and

    (vii) responses to learning experience.

The Code of Practice states that the LEA will then assess the evidence and decide whether the child's difficulties or developmental delays are likely to be resolved only through a multi-professional approach which will require monitoring and review over a period of time (paragraph 5.19). In fact, this guidance is not particularly helpful. More helpful is the consideration of special educational provision (paragraph 5.23) and the description of a developmental programme for younger children (paragraph 5.6).

The basic test should be whether the children have severe or complex needs so that the statutory procedures are necessary at this young age in order to maximise their opportunities for the future, prevent lack of development or reduce the handicap or problem. Non-educational services at this age are likely to be essential.

It is however to be remembered that such non-education staff do not necessarily supply non-educational provision. Speech therapy is likely to be educational as well as non-educational and in cases of more severe disability, occupational therapy and physiotherapy will be as much educational as they will be medical.

The parental right to express a preference for a maintained school to be named in the statement is stressed in the Code of Practice. Parents are likely to regard this as important, as they will see the provision of the statement for a very young child as the first part of the child's future developmental plan. The existence of an appropriate school once a child is of compulsory school age is going to be an important factor in any parental considerations, as it will be for the LEA itself in planning for the future.

For these very young children, access to specialised help is going to be an important part of the special educational provision. Access to a home-based learning programme and the services of a peripatetic teacher for the hearing or visually impaired in those cases will be the help required. Equally, for those who have speech impairments which constitute either the major problem or an associated part of their problems, the importance of speech therapy cannot be underestimated.

The services working within a local authority with young children, including home-based learning programmes, should be clearly specified in the statement, together with the arrangements for the provision made by the local education authority. Parents should be able to understand the statement, and what help is actually being offered and intended to be given. Where services are provided under the Children Act, whether because the child is on the child protection register or more likely because the child is defined as disabled within the terms of section 17(10) of the Children Act, the social services are obliged to provide statutory assistance. It is important that the LEA and the social services department should jointly agree arrangements and ensure there is a proper plan for provision for all the child's needs, including those which are non educational. In some instances children under five will have received considerable support without a statement. This could well be even though the provision is sufficient to justify a statement in the cases of children of compulsory school age.

If a child requires a statement prior to entering primary school at the age of five, careful attention should be paid to the parent's views and information available from all relevant sources. Particular attention is required to be given to the child's health and development and home environment to ensure that learning difficulties do not relate to wider family problems, in order to promote appropriate support for parents.

This is an area in which it is anticipated that considerable difficulties lie ahead for local education authorities. Many local authorities do have a statement in force at the time the child with obvious disabilities enters primary school. However, many other authorities have failed to implement such a system and in many cases children do not obtain statements of special educational needs until some time after entering the school system; in some cases it has been years. The Code should have an effect here.

In such cases parents are entitled to insist on the statement and would be well advised to make sure they obtain a statement by requesting an assessment. Where the child is of compulsory school age, despite the fact that the authority may be intending to assess a child's needs, and there will be no question that a statement of special educational needs will eventually be supplied, parents may well wish to request a statutory assessment themselves. This will enforce the time limits set out in the chapter dealing with statements and the assessment regulations, and ensure that adequate provision including non-educational provision is made to meet the child's needs.

If the child requires speech therapy and does not have it at school, or does not have adequate speech therapy, it is obviously advisable that the parents request a statutory assessment in order to ensure that adequate speech therapy is available. The same comment applies to occupational therapy and physiotherapy, and also to all children who require specialist help by specialist teachers or from other sources.

ARRIVAL AT PRIMARY SCHOOL

For those children who do arrive at an ordinary primary school, even those who may have had considerable help already but no statement, it is important that the parents liaise with the head teacher, and the relevant school staff to obtain an assessment of the child's special educational needs, if this is either arguably or certainly required.

The Code of Practice (in paragraph 5.29) draws the attention of schools to the need to assess pupil's current levels of attainment on entry in order to ensure they build upon their earlier years. Where a child is identified as having or potentially having a special educational need, the head teacher, the SEN co-ordinator and the child's class teacher should:

1. Use information arising from the child's early years experiences to provide starting points for curricular development for the child.

2. Identify and focus attention on the child's skills and highlight areas for early action to support the child within the class.

3. Take appropriate action for example, developing in an individual education plan, and monitoring and evaluating strategies to maximise development and alert any relevant support or external professionals at the earliest possible age.

4. Ensure that ongoing observations and assessment provides regular feedback to teachers and parents about a child's achievement and experiences and, at the outcome of any such assessment, form the basis for planning the next steps of the child's learning.

5. Use the assessment process to allow children to show what they know, understand and can do, as well as to identify any learning difficulties.

6. Involve parents in developing and implementing learning programmes at home and in school.

The Code of Practice draws attention to the fact that where children are suffering from a developmental delay, where parents do not speak English or Welsh as a first language, they are likely to be particularly disadvantaged, if they are not identified at the earliest possible age. Equally, there is likely to be a category of pupils, where the parents have a lack of command of the English language and knowledge of the system, who may well be at the greatest disadvantage. Such parents are less likely to know about the child's statutory rights, or appreciate the full situation. In conclusion, therefore, it is probably right to observe that, even for children with severe problems, in practice the question as to whether they will be statemented prior to their coming of compulsory school age rather depends on how a local authority will operate its identification system. Parents should not lightly ignore their rights to request an assessment, as it may be very important both for the child's future development, and to reduce the extent of the child's disability.

Chapter 7

Criteria for Deciding to Make a Statement

Section 168(1) of the 1993 Act provides that where, in the light of a section 167 assessment, it is necessary for the LEA to determine the special educational provision which the child's learning difficulties calls for, the LEA shall make and maintain a statement of his or her special educational needs. The conduct of the statutory assessment, and the gathering of advice from agencies and individuals is set out in the chapter on statements. Following the receipt of the statutory advice and representations, if any, the LEA must decide whether and on what basis to draw up a statement of special educational needs. The Code of Practice deals with the criteria in Chapter 4. In Chapter 4.1 it is stated that in a small number of cases the LEA may decide that the degree of the child's learning difficulty or disability, and the nature of the provision necessary to meet this child's needs, requires the LEA to determine the child's special educational provision through making a statement.

This introduction to the making of a statement is in fact misleading, in the Code of Practice. Chapter 4 obviously follows on from the school-based assessment procedures, together with the statutory assessment of children with special educational needs. Once an LEA has arrived at the point of actually commencing an assessment, it is clear there are problems which require an assessment, and one is dealing with a child for whom in the statutory language it is necessary to make an assessment.

Once one has arrived at this point, under the old system the LEA normally expected a statement and under the new system one would expect that once an assessment is commenced, it is likely to be concluded that a statement is necessary.

The words of the statute in section 168(1) are 'it is necessary for the LEA to determine the special educational provision which the child's learning difficulty calls'. Whether it is necessary or not will depend on the facts of the case. Often, the answer will be that the LEA is required to maintain a statement due to the fact that special educational provision, over and above that available to the child in the mainstream school, is required. However, the Code of Practice is again somewhat vague on this issue.

In *R -v- The Secretary of State for Education and Science ex parte* W Transcript 27/5/94, Mr. Justice Harrison pointed out that the Secretary of State, in determining appeals under section 8, must be satisfied that the provision is actually available to meet the child's needs and is not theoretically available (pg. 12D to 14C). In that case the Secretary of State was satisfied that in theory the provision set out in the statement could be made in an ordinary maintained school, although with a statement of special educational needs, and not in a specialist school. However, the Secretary of State was not satisfied on the evidence that the ordinary maintained school could actually deliver and make available that provision to the child.

Although the decision was under section 8 of the 1981 Act, the principle is no different. At the point when the LEA is deciding to make a statement, the law has not changed. Whether the help is actually there to make the provision is, in fact, important.

The Code of Practice fails to address the point as to whether or not the provision is actually available in mainstream school or mainstream schools in the area. Chapter 4.2 fails to address the practical point as to whether it actually is available. As the Code in its Introduction does not expect to be applied all at once, this omission is significant.

Equally, the mainstream school may not make available provision or may, in fact, have reasonably decided to budget elsewhere. On a practical basis, although all mainstream schools are funded for special educational needs, the question arises of whether they can deal with all disabilities, even all disabilities which can be met in theory, in a mainstream school. The Code concentrates on theory; it is not actually addressing the question of whether the help is actually there.

However, the Code of Practice also rightly points out in Chapter 4.4 that where funds are delegated to schools for a particular purpose of making a specialist provision for a child who would normally be the subject of a statement, the fact that it has such a delegated budget and therefore has the special funds does not mean that the statement should not be made. Equally, in the same paragraph the Code of Practice points out that even where additional funds, or provision in other ways, are not going to be made available, a child may require multi-disciplinary involvement and monitoring through the annual review process and other means so as to need a statement. Good examples of this are cases of children who are suffering from the effects of abuse. They may have developed considerable problems and are at risk, but require no other provision.

A decision not to make a statement following the assessment of a child's needs is now subject to an appeal, the details of which will be considered in the chapter on appeals. Previously, such appeals were not directly against a refusal to make a statement but were expressed slightly differently under the 1981 Education Act, and were in writing to the Secretary of State. In some cases, refusals of statements or indeed assessments were not properly justified by LEAs. The Code of Practice draws the LEA's attention to the following issues on the child's learning difficulties:

1. Is the information about the child that emerges from the assessment broadly in accordance with the evidence presented by the school for consideration by the LEA?

2. If not, are there aspects of the child's needs which the school may have overlooked or has overlooked, and with the benefit of advice, minor help or equipment could be effectively addressed by the school within its own resources.

3. With regard to the child's special educational provision:

    (i) Do the proposals for the child's special educational provision which emerge from statutory assessment indicate that special educational provision being made by the school is appropriate for the child's needs.

    (ii) If not, are there approaches, with the benefit of advice, equipment or other minor provision that means the school could effectively adopt within its own resources, and without further monitoring, the benefit of the child.

These questions are, of course, helpful, but the best and most accurate guide for a parent, or any advisor, whether working within local authorities or for parents, is to approach special needs in a consistent manner.

1. What are the child's educational needs; what is the diagnosis? A list should be compiled. Please remember it is the education need not any medical cause that is a need.

2. What is the provision to meet the needs? A list should be compiled.

3. Is it available at the child's ordinary school?

The next question is whether that provision can be made by the ordinary school, but whether it ought to be made by the ordinary school without a multi-disciplinary approach or oversight by an educational psychologist or other expert.

This more basic approach really addresses the whole child, and whether or not the provision is there. It is a practical approach to this decision. In addition, if the school has not properly assessed the child's problems and needs, parents will need to be satisfied that it can and will in the future do so. While a failure in the past is not evidence of future failure, it is good reason to be very careful before deciding the school can continue on its own without assistance and without a statement.

When considering whether a statement should be made, and whether to make an appeal, parents would be well advised to bear in mind the words of Lord Justice Slade in *R -v- Surrey County Council ex parte H*, 83 LGR at pg. 219 where he pointed out that LEAs were not bound to make the best or a utopian provision for children with special educational needs. While that is true, it must be effective, and it must work. Bearing in mind that these decisions are now subject to an appeal, the LEAs will have to prove on the facts that the school is able to make an effective provision without a statement of special educational needs.

In practice, one would normally expect a statement to be made for a child with a severe or complex learning difficulty. This was good guidance when in the draft Code of Practice and for some reason has been abandoned in the final Code of Practice.

The guidance given in paragraph 10 of Chapter 4 of the Code, namely, that if the assessment and provision made by the school are appropriate but the child is nonetheless not progressing or not progressing sufficiently well, the LEA should consider what further provision may be needed and what provision can be made within the school's resources, is too limited in the light of the above criteria. One would normally expect a child failing to progress within such provision or not progressing sufficiently well to have greater problems or undetected problems.

The examples given for drawing up a statement, that the LEA conclude that a child requires:

1. Regular direct teaching by a specialist teacher.

2. Daily individual support from a non-teaching assistant.

3. A significant piece of equipment such as a closed circuit TV, computer, CD-Rom Device with appropriate ancillaries and software.   •

4. Major building adaptation such as the installation of a lift.

5. A regular involvement and non educational agencies.

These are reasonable examples. The Code states that the LEA may conclude that the school could not reasonably be expected to make such provision within its own resources; in such cases the nature of the provision suggests that the LEA should formally identify in the statement of the child's needs the full range of provision to be made and the review arrangements which will apply. The LEA's conclusions will, of course, depend on the precise circumstances of the case.

The essential question is whether the provision is available and will be made, and if it is not to ensure that somebody is responsible for making it. It is therefore anticipated that, on the facts, an LEA will lose an appeal if a school is unable or unwilling to make provision.

If the LEA concludes that a change of placement may be indicated and the change involves moving to a mainstream school, to the specialist unit even at the same school, or a new mainstream school in the area of another, then the LEA are directed in the Code to consider drawing up a statement. If such a move is necessary, this amounts to a determination of provision by the LEA and the Code of Practice is giving good guidance on this issue.

Lastly, LEAs are directed to consider the disruption of frequent moves where children have parents who work in the Armed Forces so that their education will be significantly disrupted.

The Code of Practice suggests that statements should not be necessary in cases where the LEA conclude that the child's needs call for:

1. Occasional advice to the school from the external specialist.

2. Occasional support with personal care from a non-teaching assistance.

3. Access to a particular piece of equipment such as a portable word processing device, an electronic keyboard and tape recorder.

4. Minor building alterations.

In general again, this is good practical advice.

The Code of Practice also recognises the right to make assessments in an emergency and emergency placements. The author agrees with the guidance given, in Chapter 4, paragraphs 4.13 to 4.16. These will be exceptional cases.

Chapter 8

What is a Statement?

The 1981 Education Act introduced the new concept of a statement of a child's special educational needs. In so doing Parliament adopted the recommendation of the Warnock Report CMND7212, the report of the Committee of Enquiry into the Education of Handicapped Children and Young People. The Warnock Committee recommended that it was agreed that special help and protection was necessary for children with the more severe or complex special educational needs. For that purpose a statement of special educational needs was the recommended method of assisting the child.

As noted in Chapter 5, the Warnock report estimated that, nationally, as many as 20 per cent of children have special educational needs for which some additional provision might be made at some time in their school career, from within or outside the resources of the ordinary school. Of this 20 per cent the Warnock Committee estimated that 2 per cent would be within the category of children who would require statements.

Essentially, therefore, a statement is intended to protect in practice children with the more severe or complex type of problem. However, neither the 1981 nor the 1993 Acts set out guidelines for such a test and, as will be considered later, the word 'necessary' which is the word used in the 1993 statute in all the relevant sections certainly requires a judgment concerning the terms of the applicable section at each stage of the statutory powers. For example, it may well be necessary to make a statement in the case of a child with a less severe difficulty in order to ensure that the child is given proper special educational provision, if it is not available to that child. Alternatively, it may be necessary to assess but not to make a statement. As considered in Chapter 2 the legal definition (see pp.12–13) clearly depends on the facts of each case.

Obviously, a child with a problem which is less severe will soon become a child with a severe problem, if no help is given or if inadequate help is given. In addition, it must be appreciated that the overall estimate of 20 per cent included children who have been ill, children who have problems at home such as a divorce, children who are slow at some subjects, and children who do have identifiable and definable problems which are capable of categorisation such as dyslexia, (specific learning difficulties), autism, or emotional or behavioural problems.

It is, however, of interest that it is the 2 per cent group that has been the subject of consideration rather than the wider group who made up the figure of 20 per cent. In order to consider the nature of a statement, it is first necessary to consider how a statement is compiled. In this chapter it is the mechanical process of assessment that is considered, not why an assessment is made.

A statement of special educational needs requires an assessment of the child's needs under section 167. In section 167 the test is whether the local authority is of the opinion that the child for whom they are responsible falls, or probably falls, within the criteria in sub-section 2. The criteria in section 167(2) provides that a child falls within this sub-section if:

(a) he has special educational needs, and

(b) it is necessary for the authority to determine the special educational provision which any learning difficulty he may have calls for.

If this is the case, the authority is required to serve a notice on the child's parents informing them:

(a) that they propose to make an assessment of the child's special educational needs;

(b) of the procedure to be followed in making the assessment;

(c) of the name of the officer of the authority from whom further information may be obtained; and

(d) of the parent's right to make representations and submit written evidence. The period during which these may be made cannot be less than 29 days or more than the period specified in the notice.

If, having served the notice, and having taken into account parental representations, the authority is still of the opinion that the child falls or probably falls within sub-section 2, the authority is bound to make an assessment of the child's needs.

An assessment must be made in statutory form. The process of assessment gives careful consideration to all aspects of the child's needs. It requires the authority to obtain professional advice from a number of sources, as defined in the Education (Special Educational Needs) Regulations 1994, SI No 1047, pp.167–190, Appendix 6.

THE PROCESS OF ASSESSMENT

The first step is to inform the parents. This applies, however, once the assessment is commenced. Regulation 5 of the 1994 assessment regulations provides for the service of notice on a child's parents of a proposal to make an assessment either under section 167 or, in the case of a child at grant maintained school under section 174(2). Having given notice to the parents, the LEA must send copies of the relevant notice to:

(a) the social services authority;

(b) the district health authority; and

(c) if the child is registered at school, the head teacher of the school.

The notice served must describe to the recipient what help the authority is likely to request (Regulation 5(2)).

SERVICE OF DOCUMENTS IN AN ASSESSMENT

Documents and notices required to be served under Part 3 of the Act or Regulations may be served or sent, or a notice may be given by properly addressing, pre-paying and posting a letter containing any such document or notice.

Regulation 4(2) defines the proper address of a person as:

(a) In the case of a child's parents, his last known address.

(b) In the case of the head teacher and other members of staff at the school, the school's address.

(c) In the case of any other person, the last known address of the place where he carried on business, his profession or other employment.

Where first class post is used, the document or notice is treated as served, sent or given on the second working day after the date of the posting, unless the contrary is shown. If, therefore, it is contended that service has not been effected, there is a presumption that it was effected two days after it was served, sent or given.

The burden of proof to show it was not served, sent or given is upon the party who is alleging a failure of service. In addition, the regulation stipulates that the date of posting shall be presumed (unless the contrary is shown to be the case) to be the date of the post mark on the envelope containing the document.

ADVICE TO BE SOUGHT

The authority is required by Regulation 6 to seek the following advice:

(a) from the child's parent;

(b) educational advice is provided for in Regulation 7;

(c) medical advice from a district health authority is provided for in Regulation 8;

(d) psychological advice is provided for in Regulation 9;

(e) advice from Social Services;

(f) any other advice that the authority considers appropriate for the purpose of arriving at a satisfactory assessment.

Regulation 6(2) provides that the advice shall be written advice relating to:

(a) the educational, medical, psychological or other features of the case (according to the nature of the advice sought) which appear to be relevant to the child's educational needs (including his likely future needs);

(b) how those features could affect the child's educational needs, and

(c) the provision which is appropriate for the child in light of those features of the child's case, whether by way of special educational provision or non-educational provision, but not relating to any matter which is required to be specified in a statement by virtue of section 168(4).

CONSULTATION

Regulation 6(3) states that the person from whom the advice is sought can, in connection with this, consult such persons as it appears to him expedient to consult, and he shall also consult such persons, if any, as are specified in a particular case by the authority as persons who have the relevant knowledge or information relating to the child.

The expert from whom the advice is sought has, therefore, a discretion, if it appears to him expedient to consult some other person. The local education authority has power to specify that a consultation should take place.

In seeking the advice from the relevant expert specified in Regulation 6(1) the local education authority is required by Regulation 6(4) to provide the person with copies of the following:

(a) Representations made by the parent; and

(b) Any evidence submitted by, or at the request of, the parent under section 167(1)(d).

REASSESSMENT

If the authority is conducting a reassessment, it is not required to seek educational advice, medical advice, psychological advice, advice from social services or any other advice considered necessary, if they have obtained advice within the preceding 12 months and are satisfied, as a local education authority, that they themselves, the person who gave the advice, and the child's parents are satisfied that the existing advice is sufficient.

If, therefore, there is a reassessment within a short period of time, the only obligation on the authority is to seek parental advice and here Regulation 6(5) applies. However, the authority could, under this regulation, be required to obtain some but not all of the earlier advice.

EDUCATIONAL ADVICE

The authority is obliged by Regulation 7 to seek advice from a qualified teacher. Regulation 7(i) specifies that the following advice shall be sought.

- (a) from the head teacher of each school which the child is currently attending or which he has attended at any time within the preceding 18 months;

- (b) if advice cannot be obtained from a head teacher of a school which the child is currently attending (because the child is not attending a school or otherwise) from a person whom the authority are satisfied has experience of teaching children with special educational needs or knowledge of the differing provision which may be called for in different cases to meet those needs;

- (c) if the child is not currently attending a school and if advice obtained under sub-paragraph (b) is not advice from such a person responsible for educational provision for him; and

- (d) if any of the child's parents is a serving member of Her Majesty's armed forces, from the Service Children's Education Authority.

The Authority (as a result of medical advice or otherwise) may have reason to believe that the child is either hearing impaired, visually impaired or both. If the educational advice in paragraph 7(1) comes from a teacher not qualified to teach pupils who are impaired in this way, then the advice sought must be given after consultation of a person who is so qualified (Regulation 7(5)).

MEDICAL ADVICE (REGULATION 8)

Medical advice is required to be sought from the district health authority who must obtain the advice from a fully registered medical practitioner. In practice, a specifically designated medical officer normally gives such advice.

PSYCHOLOGICAL ADVICE (REGULATION 9)

Psychological advice is provided for in Regulation 9. Such advice shall be sought from a person:

(a) regularly employed by the authority as an educational psychologist; or

(b) engaged by the authority as an educational psychologist in the case in question.

Regulation 9(2) provides that the advice sought from this person:

Shall, if that person has reason to believe another psychologist has relevant knowledge of, or information relating to the child, be given after consultation with that other psychologist. This power is without prejudice to the general power to consult under Regulation 6(3).

These new regulations are very similar to the 1983 Regulations. However, the major change brought about by the 1993 Act and the new regulations made under it is that they impose time limits on the process of assessments. This is a considerable reform.

THE TIMETABLE FOR THE PROCESS

The LEA initiates the process. The first task for the LEA, having notified the parents that the statutory assessment might be necessary or having received a request from the parents or a grant maintained school, is to decide whether a statutory assessment must be made. The timetable in each case is as follows:

1. The LEA concludes that it may be necessary to make a statement and serve the statutory notice giving 29 days to

make representations. Six weeks after issuing a notice under section 167(1) the LEA must tell parents whether they will or will not make a statutory assessment.

2. Parents request a statutory assessment under either 172(2) or 173(1). The LEA must decide within six weeks of receiving the request whether they will or will not make a statutory assessment and inform the parents.

3. The governing body of grant-maintained schools where there exists section 13 Direction to admit a pupil, request a statutory assessment under 174(1). The parents must be informed within 29 days at least, and the LEA must, within six weeks of receiving the request, tell the parents and the governing body whether they will or will not make a statutory assessment.

4. *Making the assessment*: the period from the LEA's decision to make the statutory assessment and the LEA's decision whether or not to make a statement must normally be no more than ten weeks.

5. *Drafting the proposed statement or a note in lieu of a statement*: the period from the LEA's decision whether to make a statement to the issue of a proposed statement or a notice of the LEA's decision not to make a statement must be within two weeks. The Code of Practice requires a note in lieu, although the Regulations do not.

6. *Finalising the statement*: the period from the issue of the proposed statement and the final copy of the statement must normally be no more than eight weeks.
Total 26 weeks.

EXCEPTIONS TO THE LIMITS

Regulations provide for the following exceptions to the time limit in Regulation 11:

(a) Having received full advice as requested by the LEA, further advice or reports are needed as a result of exceptional circumstances.

(b) Where the parents want to provide advice for an assessment after six weeks from the LEA's request.

(c) Where district health authorities or social services departments have had no relevant knowledge of the child prior to receiving a copy of the LEA's proposal to make an assessment or form notice that the child's parents have requested an assessment.

(d) Where the LEA and the district health authority or social services department are aware of exceptional personal circumstances affecting the child and his parents following the process of assessment or the making of a statement.

(e) Where the parent or child are absent from the LEA's area for a continuous period of more than four weeks.

(f) Where a child fails to attend for an appointment for an examination or test.

(g) Where the LEA issues a request for educational advice during the period beginning one week before the school closes for a continuous period of more than four weeks, ending one week before it re-opens.

(h) Where the parents, having received a proposed statement, want to make representations about the content of the statement after the 15 day period allowed for, or seek more than one meeting under paragraph 4 of Schedule 10.

(i) The LEA has sent a written request to the Secretary of State seeking his consent under section 189(5)(b) to the child being educated in an independent school which is not approved by him and such consent has not been received by the LEA within two weeks of the date on which the request was sent.

In practice, delays are likely to occur where the parents want to submit their own evidence in relation to assessing the child's needs by an independent expert, if they have not obtained expert advice in advance of the decision to assess, or where they wish to make representations in relation to the draft statement. A draft statement must be served prior to a final statement.

The diagram below represents this process visually.

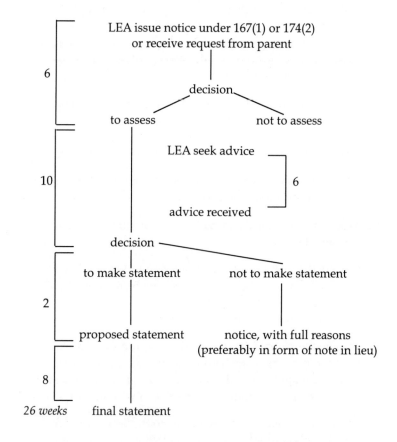

THE DRAFT STATEMENT AND THE RIGHT TO MAKE REPRESENTATIONS

Having obtained all the advice, if in the light of the assessment, or of any representations made by the child's parents (the right to make those representations are contained in Schedule 10, paragraph 4 of the Act), the LEA decides it is necessary to determine the special educational provision and any learning difficulties the child may have calls for, the authority shall make and maintain the statement of his special educational needs (section 168(1)). Having served a draft statement, the next step is for the parents either to accept it or to make representations.

Prior to the making of the statement in final form, the education authority is obliged to serve on the parent of the child concerned:

(a) a copy of the proposed statement; and

(b) notice explaining the arrangements made in paragraphs 3 and 4 of Schedule 10 and the right to appeal under section 170 concerning any other further information Schedule 10 paragraph 2.

The copy of the proposed statement shall not specify any matters specified in section 168(4). This means that the type of school or institution, the name of the school or institution, the provision at the school or institution is not specified. The reason for this is to give the parents an opportunity to express a preference for a particular school or type of school. Under Schedule 10 (paragraphs 3 and 4) the parent has the right to express a preference for a choice of school, and also the right to make representations about the proposed statement.

Schedule 10 paragraph 4(1) gives the parent the right to make representations or further representation to the local education authority about the contents of the statement and requires the authority to arrange a meeting between him and an officer of the authority at which the statement can be discussed.

Having attended a meeting arranged under Schedule 10, Sub-paragraph 4(1)(b) a parent can, if he disagrees with part of an assessment, require the authority to arrange the meeting or meetings such as is considered necessary, to enable the parent to discuss the relevant advice with the appropriate person.

RELEVANT ADVICE

Relevant advice means advice given to the authority in connection with the assessment which they consider to be relevant to that part of the assessment with which the parent disagrees. In Paragraph 4(3), 'an appropriate person' means the person who gave the relevant advice or any other person who, in the opinion of the authority, is the appropriate person to discuss it with the parent. This means the authority can in appropriate cases field a substitute.

Representations requested under Sub-paragraph 4(1)(a) must be made within 15 days, beginning with the date the written notice is served on the parent, or, if meetings have been arranged, the date fixed for that meeting or the last of those meetings.

Where representations are made to the authority under paragraph 4(1)(a), the authority shall not make a statement until they have considered the representations and the period, or the last of the periods, allowed by paragraph 4 has expired.

Where the statement has been subject to representations, it may be made in the form proposed except for the matters to be excluded from the copy of the proposed statement or in a form modified in the light of representations.

CHOICE OF SCHOOL

Schedule 10, paragraph 3 again makes a major clarification in the rights of parents in relation to the legislation. Under the 1981 Act, there was doubt as to whether a parent could in fact appeal the issue of an appropriate school. The Minister took the view in Circular 22/89 that the school was part and parcel of the provision. This was a most sensible line to take.

Paragraph 3 of Schedule 10 requires every local authority to make arrangements to enable the parent on whom a copy of the proposed statement has been served to express a preference as to a maintained, grant-maintained, or grant-maintained special school at which he wishes education to be provided for his child, and to give reasons for his preference (Paragraph 3(1)).

Any preference must be expressed within 15 days beginning:

(a) with a date on which written notice is required to be served by paragraph 2(b) is served with a copy of the proposed statement; or

(b) the meeting or meetings has or have been arranged under paragraph 4(1)(b) or 4(2) and the date fixed for those meetings and the last of those meetings has expired.

By paragraph 3(3) of Schedule 10 where a local education authority makes a statement in a case where the parent has expressed the preference, the LEA is obliged to specify the named school unless:

(a) the school is unsuitable to the child's age, ability or aptitude or his special educational needs; or

(b) the attendance at the school would be incompatible with the provision of efficient education for children with whom he would be educated or the efficient use of resources.

Where the local education authority are required to specify the name of any maintained or grant-maintained school (special or not) it must consult the governing body of the school, or if the school is maintained by another local authority, that authority, before specifying the school.

THE FINAL STATEMENT

Drawing the statement together

The statement contains the assessment of a child's special educational needs. Regulation 10 provides all matters to be taken into account in making assessment which are then used to make the statement. They are:

(a) Any representations made by the child's parents under section 167(1)(d).

(b) Any evidence submitted by or at the request of the child's parents under section 167(1)(d); and

(c) The advice obtained by the LEA under Regulation 6. These matters go into the draft statement, and thereafter the statement can be withdrawn, changed, reconsidered, and then issued in final form.

By section 168(2) the statement must be in such form and contain such information as may be prescribed. By section 168(3)(a) in particular the statement shall give details of the authority's assessment of a child's special educational needs; and

Specify the special educational provision to be made for meeting those needs section 168(3).

The following additional matters must be specified:

(a) The type of school or other institution which the local authority considers would be appropriate for the child;

(b) If they are not required under Schedule 10 to specify the name of any school in the statement, specify the name of any school or institution whether in the UK or elsewhere which they consider would be appropriate for the child; and

(c) Specify the provision for the child for which they make arrangements under section 163 which they consider should be specified in the statement (section 168(4)).

Thus far, the statutory procedure and requirements of Regulation, if looked at strictly, could be misleading, in that it could fail to define a child or young person.

The nature of a statement, and its purpose was considered in *R -v- The Secretary of State for Education ex parte E* 1992 1 FLR at pg. 377. The leading judgment in the Court of Appeal Balcombe L J endorsed the approach in Nolan L. J. and the Court below delivered unanimous judgment to the Court of Appeal in adopting the words of the Judge below:

> 'The statement is no ordinary form. Part 2 may be compared to a medical diagnosis and Part 3 to a prescription for the needs diagnosed...' pg. 387G to 388H

> 'The statement looks at the *whole child*.' per Balcombe L J. pg. 388F

The Code of Practice gives guidance on the format of the statement:

Part 1   *Introduction* The child's name and address and date of birth. The child's home language and religion. The names and address(es) of the child's parents.

Part 2   *Special Educational Needs* (learning difficulties). Details of each and every one of the child's special educational needs as identified by the LEA during statutory assessment and on the advice received and attached as appendices to the statement.

Part 3   *Special Educational Provision* The special educational provision which the LEA consider necessary to meet the child's special educational needs.

> (a) The *objectives* which the special educational provision should aim to meet.

(b) The *special educational provision* which the LEA
consider appropriate to meet the needs specified
in Part 2 and to meet the specified objectives.

(c) The arrangements to be made for monitoring
progress in meeting those objectives, particularly
for setting short-term targets for the child's
progress and for reviewing his or her progress
on a regular basis.

Part 4　*Placement* The type and name of school where the
special educational provision specified in Part 3 is to
be made or the arrangements for the education to be
made otherwise than in school.

Part 5　*Non-Educational Needs* All relevant non-educational
needs of the child as agreed between the health
services, social services or other agencies and the
LEA.

Part 6　*Non-Educational Provision* Specification of relevant
non-educational provision required to meet the
non-educational needs of the child as agreed between
the health services and/or social services and the
LEA, including the agreed arrangements for its
provision.

Signature and date

APPENDICES

(Regulation 13 and Part B of the Schedule to the Regulations)

The advice appended to the statement must include:

1. Parental representations, evidence and advice

2. Educational advice

3. Medical advice

4. Psychological advice

5. Social services advice

6. Any other advice, such as the views of the child, which the
LEA or any other body from whom advice is sought consider

desirable. In particular, where the child's parent is a serving member of the armed forces, advice from the Service Children's Education Authority (SCEA).

(Regulation 13)

In short, Part 2 of the statement must address all the identified in determining needs, and Part 3 must make provision to meet each and every need. It must deal with the whole child as the Court of Appeal stated in *R -v- The Secretary of State ex parte E* supra, and be readable and intelligible by all who have to deal with a child, including a child's parents. It is a personal record of the child, and it is reviewed annually and may therefore change. There must, however, be a clear determination of the help required to meet the child's needs, and this must be usable by all required to make the provision for the child's problems.

KEEPING DISCLOSURE AND TRANSFER OF STATEMENTS

Regulation 19 of the Education Special Educational Needs Regulations 1994 provides that a statement should not be disclosed without the consent of the child's parents, except for certain statutory purposes or in the interests of the child.

Those statutory purposes obviously include an appeal to the Tribunal, and to the Secretary of State if a complaint is made to him under the 1944 Education Act. Disclosure may be made by the order of a Court or for the purposes of any criminal proceedings, for the purposes of investigations under the Local Government Act 1974 by the Local Government Commissioner, and to enable the authority to perform its duties as a result of the Disabled Persons (Services, Consultation and Representation) Act 1986, the Chronically Sick and Disabled Persons Act or the Children Act 1989, and to inspection teams as part of their inspections of the school.

In practice, obviously a statement must be disclosed to the school and child's teachers, and the LEA may also give access to persons engaged in research of special educational needs on condition the researchers do not publish anything derived from or contained in the statement which will identify the child or the child's parents.

The school governing body should have access to a child's statement, commensurate with their duties towards pupils with special educational needs. A statement is a confidential document at all times, and parties to whom disclosure is made are not entitled to breach that confidentiality. Equally, social services or health agencies who are involved in the provision in the statement can be given disclosure of a statement.

TRANSFER OF STATEMENTS

Where a child moves from one area to another area, the old authority must now transfer the statement to the new authority (Regulation 18(2)). From the date of transfer, the following matters take effect:

(a) The statement is treated on that date as the statement made by the new authority, that authority has the same duties under Part III of the 1993 Act as the first authority who made the statement.

(b) Within six weeks of the date of transfer the new authority must serve a notice on the child's parents informing him:

   (i) That the statement has been transferred.

   (ii) Whether they propose to make an assessment under 167; and

   (iii) Whether they propose to review the statement in accordance with paragraph 4.

   (iv) It follows that the new authority can accept the statement in its entirety or decide to make a completely new assessment or take a mid course and review the statement.

   (v) If the authority decide to review this statement, they can do so within 12 months of the beginning of the making of the statement, or the previous review, or within three months of the date of transfer.

   (vi) Where due to the transfer the new authority comes under a duty to arrange the child's attendance at a school specified in the statement at which, due to the move, attendance is no longer practical, the new authority may arrange for attendance at another school appropriate for the child until such time as it is possible to amend the statement in accordance with paragraph 10 of Schedule 10 of the Act.

These are important changes. The old regulations were both unclear and muddled. The statement now must be transferred, and the new authority can accept the statement for the time being, obviously subject to the statutory review period, while a shorter review period may perhaps be considered appropriate.

Chapter 9

Annual Reviews, Amending Statements and Ceasing to Maintain Statements

The three subjects of reviews of statements, amendment of statements and the decision to cease to maintain a statement ought to be considered together. In practice, they will be interlinked. The 1993 Act substantially changes the provisions dealing with reviews, and decisions to cease to maintain statements. Only in relation to amendments does the law remain effectively the same, although it is to be expected that the changes in the provisions governing reviews will, in fact, result in more frequent consideration of amendments.

THE ANNUAL REVIEW

The local education authority must review a statement within 12 months of making a statement or (as the case may be) of the previous review; and also on the making of the assessment under section 167 for a child who already has a statement 172(5). The regulations made under the provisions of section 172(1) are contained in Part 3 of the Education (Special Educational Needs) Regulations 1994, S.I. 1047. Reviews of statements are governed by Regulations 15 and 16. Regulation 15 deals with reviews of statements where the child is not yet aged 14 and attends school. Regulation 16 deals with reviews of statements where a child aged 14 attends school. Regulation 17 deals with the other cases of children who do not attend school.

The introduction of detailed procedures which are mandatory, for purposes of annual reviews, is a considerable reform. Also new is the division of a review into three categories.

LEAs have the power to review a statement at any time during the year. The Code of Practice recommends that LEAs should aim to secure the agreement of the school and the child's parents before exercising the power of review, and thus conduct the review at a time appropriate for all parties. However, they are under a mandatory duty to review all statements on an annual basis.

The Code of Practice suggests that the timing of annual reviews should reflect the circumstances of the child and the action which may flow from the review. For example, it is appropriate to conduct an annual review before a child moves to secondary school and not afterwards. The timing of the review should also reflect the circumstances and organisation of the school.

Obviously, if a school is attempting to conduct annual reviews on all statemented children at the same time, problems will undoubtedly follow.

THE PURPOSE OF AN ANNUAL REVIEW

The purpose of an annual review is to check on the effective working of the statement. The authority is required by Regulation 15(2) (in the case of children not aged 14), 16(2) (in the case of school children aged 14) and 17(2) (where they do not attend school) to obtain a written report under the regulations from the head teacher of the child's school where the child is at school, and from the authority itself where the child does not attend school. It must serve a copy of the report (which must be supplied within two months of the date given) to the child's parents.

The head teacher in the case of children at school is required to obtain advice from:

(a) The child's parents.

(b) Any person whose advice the authority consider appropriate for the purpose of arriving at a satisfactory report, and whom they specify in the notice, and any person whose advice the head teacher considers appropriate for the purpose of arriving at a satisfactory report (Regulations 15(3) and 16(3)). In the case of children not at school, the authority is required to seek advice on matters referred to in Regulation 15(4)(e), namely from any person who the authority consider appropriate (in the case of children who have attained the age of 14 who are not at school), from the child's parent or from any other person considered appropriate.

The advice required shall be written advice as to:

(a) The child's progress for meeting the objectives specified in the statement;

(b) The child's progress towards attaining any targets established in furtherance of the objectives specified in the statement;

(c) Where the school is not established in a hospital and is a maintained school, grant-maintained or grant-maintained special school, the application of the provisions of the national curriculum to the child;

(d) Where the school is not established in a hospital and is a maintained school, grant-maintained or grant-maintained special school the application of any provision substituted for the national curriculum in order to maintain a broadly balanced curriculum;

(e) Where appropriate, and in any case where a transition plan exists, any matters which are appropriate subjects of such a plan;

(f) Whether the statement is considered to be appropriate;

(g) Any amendments to the statement which would be appropriate; and

(h) Whether the authority should cease to maintain the statement.

The provisions of Regulation 15(4) apply in the same manner to children aged 14, and Regulation 17(2), with the appropriate modifications, for those who do not attend school.

The purpose of the annual review is to focus on what the child has achieved as well as any difficulties which need to be resolved. The first annual review after the child's fourteenth birthday is particularly significant in preparing for his or her transition to the further education sector and adult life. The requirements of these annual reviews are therefore directed to this future transition.

In essence, therefore, the object of an annual review is to see whether the statement is working effectively, and if it is not, what should be done, whether the statement should be changed and provision either deleted altered or amended. In some cases it is to consider whether there is a reason to cease to maintain a statement.

The regulations provide new and important rights for parents in relation to the annual review. The head teacher is required to invite the following persons to attend a meeting in relation to the annual review before the report made by the head teacher is submitted:

(a) The representative of the authority specified in the notice;

(b) The child's parents;

(c)) A member or members of the staff of the school who teach the child or who are otherwise responsible for the provision of education of the child whose attendance the head teacher considers appropriate;

(d) Any other person whose attendance the head teacher considers appropriate; and

(e) any person whose attendance the authority considers appropriate and who are specified in the notice (see Regulation 15(5)).

These provisions are slightly amended in the case of young persons aged 14 or over where the authority (by Regulation 16(3)) shall invite the following persons to attend:

(a) The child's parents;

(b) A member or members of the staff of the school who teach the child, who are otherwise responsible for the provision of education for the child, whose attendance the head teacher considers appropriate and whom he has asked the authority to invite.

(c) The representative of the social services authority;

(d) A representative or person providing career services by section 45 of the Trade Union and Employment Rights Acts 1993;

(e) Any person whose attendance the head teacher considers appropriate and whom he has asked the authority to invite; and

(f) Any person whose attendance the authority considers appropriate.

(g) Regulation 17, for young persons not at school, provides for the attendance of the child's parents where a young person is over 14, a representative of the social services authority, together with a careers services advisor under section 45 of the Trade Union and Employment Rights Act 1993, and any other person whose attendance the authority considers appropriate.

The reason for the differences in the regulation is obviously the fact that the future for those who are to go into further education or employment training needs to be considered in the case of pupils with special needs who are about to leave school. The important decision will be first whether they need to remain in school until they reach the age of 19 or whether they should leave at 16. If they need to leave at 16 because the local education authority has not appropriate provision, then the agreements with the Further and Higher Education Funding Council apply, and must be explored in detail.[*]

In the cases of children with more severe problems and young adults, the differences in section 17 reflect the individual circumstances of children and young adults who are not at school. Obviously, detailed planning for their future is needed, but the regulations reflect the much more flexible approach that is needed in these cases.

It is obvious that it is important that parents attend such meetings. If there are disagreements with the likely view of the school, parents should attend such meetings having, if possible, obtained independent professional advice such as psychologist's reports, medical reports, or other relevant reports and advice on the child or young person. Obviously, if agreement can be reached in advance and enquiries made by the parents this would be the most appropriate course.

In practice, however, these issues are most likely to concern parents (these are examples only and do not represent an exhaustive list of possibilities):

---

[*] The powers of the Council are considered in *Young Adults with Special Needs*, also by John Friel.

1. Is the statement working effectively? If the parents consider that it is not, in some cases the school will accept that more help is needed or that the young person has not made adequate progress. If, however, there are two different views on this, the parents would be well advised to come to the meeting armed with appropriate independent advice.

2. Should the statement be changed because there is a need for more or less help or simply different help to deal with problems that have emerged as a result of an increase in age of the child and different demands of the curriculum?

3. Is the authority planning adequately for further education? Has it looked properly at the Local Further and Higher Education Funding Council's provision in the area?

4. Is there good reason to cease to maintain the statement?

ANNUAL REVIEW FOR CHILDREN AT SCHOOL

The Code of Practice gives guidance on this issue in Chapter 6 particularly at paragraph 16(2), (6) to (9). As set out above, the LEA must by notice convene the meeting, giving the head teacher at least two months' notice, by the date on which the report must be submitted, and inform the head teacher who should contribute to the review. In relation to children with special needs, if there are medical or social problems, the LEA ought to consider whether the representatives of the health services or social services or both should attend such a meeting. Where under the regulations the head teacher requests information for district health authorities and social services authorities, they are required by section 166(1) to respond to the head teacher's request unless the exceptions apply. However, it will be anticipated that some problems will arise where such reports are requested.

When the evidence is received, comments on the evidence, together with an account of the review meeting, form the basis of the review report. Parental attendance at such meetings is, frankly, crucial. They should not be taken for granted. These meetings can produce surprises, and the parents should attend. The Code of Practice provides in Chapter 6 paragraph 6(15) that, where possible, pupils should be actively involved in the report process and, if appropriate, contribute to the review meeting. They should be encouraged to give their views of their progress during the previous year, discuss difficulties and share their hopes and aspirations.

The Code of Practice recognises the right of parents to bring a friend, advisor or relative or their named person, the person the LEA identify as an independent person, or maybe somebody from a voluntary organisation or parent partnership scheme to the meeting.

Where there is disagreement about progress, changes in the statement, or whether the statement should remain at all, parents obviously would be well advised to attend the meeting with as much help and information as possible to persuade all concerned of their view. This is likely to avoid future appeals. The Code of Practice requires the LEA and the school to make every effort to inform parents of their rights and responsibilities and encourage them to attend the meeting (Chapter 6 paragraph 17).

Where the child or family does not have English or Welsh as a first language, the time scale and planning for the annual review should take into account the following:

(a) Translation of the relevant documents into the family's mother tongue.

(b) To ensure that interpreters are available to the child and family both in the preparatory stages to the review meeting and at the review meeting itself.

(c) Ensure that professionals from the child's community have similar interpretations and translational facilities in order that they may contribute as fully as possible to the review process. Indeed, where possible, a bilingual support teacher and/or teacher of English or Welsh as a second language is available to the child and family.

The same principles apply where the child or their family have communication problems because of physical impairment. Each issue should be approached on the basis of the disability, and the appropriate facilities made available.

Where a child with a statement is subject to a care order, the local authority designated by the order have parental responsibility for that child. This obviously creates difficulties as to the extent of contributions to be made by the child's parents, the child's carers, residential social workers or foster parents. This should be determined by the authority in consultation with the local social services department. Such matters only apply where there is a care order.

Where care orders or education supervision orders exist, or the local authority looks after the child, the local authority social services departments should include information on the arrangements for the education of a child within its care.

The review meeting is normally expected by the Code of Practice, to take place in the child's school and to be chaired by the head teacher or the teacher who has responsibility for the school-based elements and to whom the review has been delegated. Chapter 6 of the Code paragraph 22 suggests some ten questions which should be asked at the meeting. These are perfectly sensible questions and are good guidance.

CHILDREN OTHERWISE THAN AT SCHOOL (REGULATION 17)

Where children are educated otherwise than at school (as discussed above) the regulations are effectively the same and are adapted to deal with that situation. The venue is more likely to be the LEA's offices or a hospital and will normally be chaired by a representative of the local education authority itself. In cases where there are severe medical and associated problems, the views from health services and social services will obviously be crucial. Equally, where children have been excluded from school it is important that the review takes place and produces a considered detailed plan for the child's future.

THE RESULT OF THE ANNUAL REVIEW

The annual review should record satisfactory progress or that the statement should be given a further chance to work. If this is the case, obviously no changes in this statement are necessary. If, however, the annual review shows that the child is not making adequate progress or has developed further problems or, alternatively, has made progress, the following matters are some of those that should be considered:

1. Have significant new needs emerged which are not recorded on the statement or have they been discovered?

2. Has the child's needs changed so that some of the statement is inaccurate? Are the changes due to an improvement in the child, or a change in needs, in any event?

3. Should the provision be amended to meet the child's changes in need?

4. Should the child change schools, either at the normal point of transfer (i.e. Junior to Primary), or can the child's needs be more appropriately met in a different school; for example, with a more disabled child, should they now be integrated, or should a programme of reintegration or integration be commenced?

If the basic model used by the Court of Appeal in *R -v- The Secretary of State for Education and Science* supra (1992) FLR at page 377 is followed, namely at the annual review, one should look at the needs on the statement, then see if they are correctly expressed. If the provision is appropriate, few problems will be encountered.

Finally, the meeting may record that a statement is no longer necessary.

AMENDING THE STATEMENT

Proposals to amend the statement would normally come from the annual review process. If the LEA proposes to amend a statement, whether to change the name or a school or make any other amendment, they must write to the child's parents informing them of the proposal and of their right to make representations within 15 days of receipt of the proposal. They should always explain the reason for the proposal and ensure the parents have copies of any evidence which prompted the proposal (Paragraphs 9 and 10 of Schedule 10).

The LEA must consider the representations made by the parents before deciding whether and how to amend. If they conclude an amendment should be made they must make the amendment within eight weeks of sending the letter of proposals to the parents. They must also write to the parents informing them of the decision to amend and the reasons for it, enclosing a copy of the amended statement and any relevant advice. Equally, they must inform the parents of the right of appeal. If they decide not to amend, they should write to the parents explaining why, again within eight weeks of the letter setting out the original proposals (Paragraph 10(5) of Schedule 10).

WHAT IS AN AMENDMENT?

The provisions relating to amendments of statements of special educational needs remain effectively unchanged (with some altera-tions as to the time limits) from the 1981 Act. There has been no Court decision on what constitutes an amendment.

In practice, this issue is likely to become more important, since there is now a new right of appeal. However, its importance is likely to be evidential, because if the local authority makes an amendment, which is not justified and should have been made as a result of a proper reassessment of the child's needs, a parent will normally be able to obtain proper professional evidence to show that the amend-ment has been made in an unwarranted and unprofessional manner, without proper professional advice, and that, on proper professional advice, the child has a different need. The practical importance is, therefore, for the purposes of preparation of an appeal against amended statements. An amendment is any change which does not require a full reassessment.

ISSUES INVOLVING A CHANGE OF SCHOOL

The Code of Practice devotes some consideration to this point at Chapter 6(30) to 6(33). This is due to the existence of new appeal rights, and rights given to parents who request the LEA to name a school or substitute the name of a maintained school or special schools or grant-maintained, or grant-maintained special school for the name of the school in Part 4 of the statement. (These provisions are dealt with in chapters dealing with assessments and appeals and will not be repeated here.)

It is, however, important that an annual review gives detailed and proper thought, and careful advance planning to the transition either into a special school if that is what is needed, or to integration into an ordinary school, or to transfer from primary to secondary school. Arrangements for a child's placement should be finalised in advance, and the Code of Practice recommends that this should be by the beginning of the child's last term before transfer. It is impor-tant for placements to be finalised as early as possible in order for any advance arrangements to be made, and to ensure that parents feel confident and secure about the arrangements in question. However, the Code of Practice itself fails to point out that children with special needs will often become disturbed and upset or regress to a degree if their future is uncertain. It is therefore in the child's interest to plan such transitions properly. Cases will, of course, arise when a provision breaks down and urgent action has to be taken. Such cases are exceptional.

ANNUAL REVIEWS FROM 14 TO 19

Some pupils with statements or special needs remain in school after the age of 16, some do not. The local education authority remains responsible for pupils until they are 19 (section 156(5)). Others with statements will, however, leave school at 16 and move, for example, to a college within the further education sector or, in cases of more severely disabled pupils, to social services provision. Whatever the intended further destination of the young person, the annual review has great significance as he or she approaches the age of 16.

In practical terms the significance of the annual review is also increased due to the changes brought in by the 1992 Further and Higher Education Act. If a young person leaves school and goes into the further education sector, a statement will automatically lapse and the young person no longer falls within the definition of a child with special needs for whom the local education authority are responsible under section 156.

The Further and Higher Education Funding Council has duties under section 4 of the Act to young persons with special needs and, in appropriate cases, this will include a placement at a specialist educational establishment, which may or may not include a school outside that sector.

However, it is the primary responsibility of the local education authority, when a young person has a statement, to continue that statement until the age of 19, if they require a school education. They cannot divest themselves of their responsibility for a young person simply because they have, for example, placed him at a school outside of the local educational system, and that school ends at 16, if he requires a further school with an A-level facility, R -v- Dorset CC and others ex parte Goddard co/1873/94 unreported 5/12/94.

Parents will therefore need to check carefully what provision is available in the area in such situations.

The LEA may have concentrated its forces into sixth form colleges; for example, there may be few sixth forms left in LEA control, except in voluntary or grant-maintained schools in the local area. It is therefore quite possible that, where a child requires to transfer school at 16, or to transfer to the local further education college, considerable work may be necessary to establish the existence of adequate provision and an adequate opportunity to succeed in further education.

Regulation 15(4) requires such issues to be considered, but in addition, seeks to plan for the future.

Under the Disabled Persons Services and Representation Act 1986, by section 5 as amended, the LEA must seek a determination as to whether a young person is a disabled person under the Act and whether they require services from the local authority when leaving school. It should be borne in mind that the definition of disability can include even young persons with severe dyslexia.

For this reason, the LEA must also ensure that other providers, such as social services, are aware of the annual review and the procedures to be followed, and they must invite social services departments to attend the review so that any parallel assessments of the following acts (namely, the Disabled Persons Services and Representation Act 1986, the NHS and Community Care Act 1990 and the Chronically Sick and Disabled Persons Act) can contribute to and draw information from the review process. Where children have been in the care of the local authority or accommodated by the local authority, Children Act duties continue beyond the age of 18, and Children Act assessments are equally appropriate.

The LEA must in addition invite the career service to be represented at the review meeting, to enable all options for further education, careers and occupational training to be given serious consideration. The career service will also be able to identify any specific targets which should be set as part of the annual review, and ensure that independence, training, personal social skills and other aspects of the wider curriculum are fully addressed during the young person's last years at school.

The LEA should then review the report and the transition plan after the meeting and circulate it to the young person's parents, head teachers, those from whom advice was sought, or those attending the meeting and any others the LEA consider appropriate. In particular, the LEA should consider passing the review report and transition plan to the Further Education Funding Council, particularly in cases where a decision needs to be taken about specialist college provision outside the further education sector.

The Code of Practice (in Chapter 6, paragraph 46) again lists some 16 sensible questions to be considered at the meeting. The essential object of the review is to produce a proper transition plan at the appropriate time for the young person. When it is that the time comes to move from school will obviously depend on the person, the disability or problem, and its nature.

The transition plan should be a detailed plan based on all the available evidence, including the previous annual review, and should deal with the strengths and weaknesses of the young person.

The issue of further education is considered in detail in *Young Adults with Special Needs* (Friel 1995). However, schools should be familiar with the following legislation, which is important in the case of all young persons with special needs:

(a) The Chronically Sick and Disabled Persons Act 1970.

(b) The Employment and Training Act 1973 as amended by the Trade Union Reform and Employment Rights Act 1993.

(c) The Disabled Persons (Services, Consultation and Representation Act (1986).

(d) The Children Act 1989.

(e) The National Health Service and Community Care Act 1990.

(f) The Further and Higher Education Act 1992.

Under the Children Act 1989 and the NHS and Community Care Act 1990, social services departments are required to arrange a multi-disciplinary assessment and provide care plans for children and adults with significant disabilities. These may include the provision of further educational facilities. These reviews are therefore extremely important.

Although the Code of Practice uses the word 'significant', it is obvious that even adults with a severe dyslexic problem may well require a special educational provision in further education, since the definition of disability does not exclude a severely dyslexic person. Each case should be judged on its own facts.

The Further and Higher Education Funding Council has published a circular on its responsibility in these issues, and has now agreed with local education an assessment procedure.

The circular approves the terms of the agreements between the LEAs and the FEFC, in that in practice the LEA will conduct assessments on behalf of the FEFC. Further and more specific details on these issues are given in *Young Adults with Special Needs*.

It is important that the young person be involved in the assessment and review. Chapter 6 Paragraph 6.59 and 60 of the Code of Practice deals with a number of issues personal to the young person themselves which should be considered. What is important is that the review produces a proper detailed plan for the future which is practical, personally tailored, and realistic.

THE CONCLUSION OF ALL REVIEWS

Following the conclusion of a review meeting, the head teacher submits his report to:

(a) The child's parents;

(b) The persons from whom advice was sought;

(c) The persons who are invited to attend the meeting;

(d) Any other person whom the authority considers appropriate;

(e) Any other person whom the head teacher considers appropriate (Regulation 15). For those over 16 and not at school, the provisions in the regulations are effectively the same, but adapted to particular circumstances – see regulation 16(8) and 17(8). The report must be completed within a week.

On receipt of the report, the authority is required to review the statement in the light of the report (Regulation 15(12) 16(9) and 17(9)). It is at this point that the decision about the young person's future is made. Following the making of a decision the authority is required, within one week, to serve copies of recommendations and any transition plan or the result of the review to the persons who attended the meeting and to whom the head teacher has submitted his report.

CEASING TO MAINTAIN A STATEMENT

A decision to cease to maintain a statement can come about as a result of a reassessment, but this is highly unlikely to happen, because the authority must consider the statement necessary in order to conduct a reassessment. Therefore it is likely that, for practical purposes, it will result from a review.

As a matter of law, a statement remains in force until an LEA ceases to maintain it, or the child is no longer the responsibility of the LEA (under section 156), where the child leaves school or goes into further education. Alternatively, if the child moves to another area, the statement will become the responsibility of another authority but the statement will not cease.

The LEA may cease to maintain a statement only if they believe that it is no longer necessary for the LEA to maintain it. The Code of Practice points out that there should be no assumption that, once the LEA have made a statement, they should maintain the statement until they are no longer responsible for the young person – see Chapter 6, paragraph 37. Statements should only be maintained where necessary and the language of section 168(1) makes this clear. However, the Code of Practice sensibly points out a decision to cease to maintain a statement should be made only after careful consideration by the LEA of all the circumstances of the case and after close consultation with the parents. The Code of Practice directs the LEA to consider the results of recent annual reviews and to consider whether the objectives of the statement have been achieved, and whether the child's needs can be met in future without the need for continuing LEA oversight.

The Code goes on to say that the LEA should always therefore consider, notwithstanding the achievement of some, or even all, the objectives in the statement, whether the child's progress will be halted or reversed if the special educational provision specified in the statement or in a modified form still required in the statement was not made. If so a statement will still be 'really needed.'

In general, the Code of Practice provides very sensible guidance on this issue. Statements are not made unless children have a problem which justifies a statement. Severe and complex learning difficulties are not normally instantly cured. It is true that different considerations will apply to some emotional and behavioural problems, but if they are severe enough to obtain a statement, they may well continue to justify the oversight of the LEA at the very least.

For most children who are the subject of a statement, there is an inherent condition requiring the statement and the provision. That condition can, of course, be alleviated or minimised but in few cases will it be cured. A dyslexic cannot be cured, for example, although teaching and experience can teach the child to avoid the problem and other skills are used in order to maximise potential. The fact, therefore, that a child achieves and makes progress does not mean that in the absence of provision of the type provided in a statement a child will progress. Indeed, in many cases, the child's condition remains and there is a requirement for support in order to continue progress. In the absence of that support, progress will often not be made, and regression will take place.

The right of appeal granted when such a decision is made, which will be considered in the later chapter on appeals, is an important reform.

Chapter 10

Rights of Appeal

The new Tribunal set up under the 1993 Act commenced existence on the 1st September 1994. The Tribunal has a legally qualified President and two lay members. The Tribunal is established by section 177 of the Act, which provides for a President of the Tribunal, and panel of persons who may serve as Chairman of the Tribunal, who are legally qualified and appointed by the Lord Chancellor, and a panel of persons who may serve as Lay Members who are appointed by the Department for Education (DFE). Section 180 provides for the setting up of rules of procedure in the Tribunal.

RIGHTS OF APPEAL

The rights of appeal, in essentially logical order, as created by the 1993 Act, are as follows:

1. Against the LEA's refusal to make an assessment following a request for the parents to assess a child's special educational needs under section 173. The Tribunal's powers on hearing such an appeal are to:

    (a) Dismiss the appeal; or

    (b) Order the LEA to arrange for an assessment to be made. Section 173(3).

2. Against the refusal of the LEA to reassess a child who has a statement under section 172(2). The Tribunal's powers are to:

    (a) Dismiss the appeal; or

    (b) Order the LEA to arrange for a reassessment to be made, section 172(4).

3. Against the LEA's refusal to make a statement for a child under section 169 of the Act. The Tribunal's powers are:

    (a) To dismiss the appeal.

    (b) To order the LEA to make and maintain a statement.

    (c) Remit the case to the LEA for reconsideration in the light of the Tribunal's observations, to consider whether a statement is necessary.

4. Against the LEA's assessment of a child's special educational needs, the provision specified in the statement of special educational needs, or if no school is named in the statement, that fact under section 170. This appeal includes decisions to amend statements and, where the LEA has reassessed, a decision to refuse to amend the statement, section 170(1) (B) and (C). The Tribunal's powers are to:

    (a) Dismiss the appeal.

    (b) Order the LEA to amend the statement, as regards needs, provision and make any consequential amendments.

    (c) Order the LEA to cease to maintain a statement section 170(3).

5. Against the LEA's decision not to change the name of a school specified in Part IV of the statement under paragraph 8 of schedule 2. The Tribunal's powers are:

    (a) To dismiss the appeal.

    (b) To order the LEA to name in the statement the school or other institutions specified by the parent, schedule 10 paragraph 8(4).

6. Against the decision of the LEA to cease to maintain a statement under Paragraph 11 of schedule 10. The Tribunal's powers are to:

    (a) Dismiss the appeal.

    (b) Order the LEA to continue to maintain a statement even in its existing form or with amendments, paragraph 11(3) of schedule 10.

In all such cases the LEA must serve a notice of their decision and inform the parents of their right of appeal.

CONSIDERATION OF SOME OF THE LIKELY ISSUES ON THESE APPEALS

1. A refusal to make an assessment (section 173). The question is whether the parents can establish that it is necessary for the authority to assess the child's special educational needs. This depends on the facts. If the advice earlier on in this work on the preparation of expert reports and the preparation of a request for an assessment has been followed, the parental case should be properly prepared at this point.

   If this is not the case, the parents will need to consider whether they need supporting evidence from the school, or an outside expert. It would be wise if the expert who compiled a report can be actually asked to come and give evidence at the tribunal, as well as the parents.

Obviously, the Code of Practice is likely to be of importance in such issues. Parents and advocates for both sides should not get obsessed by the Code of Practice. The issues will be in general as follows:

(a) Can the school manage with its own resources, or with extra help in a way that does not require a statement to make provision for the child's needs?

(b) Is the school the appropriate place to make such provision, or has it made so many mistakes that it cannot be trusted?

(c) Alternatively, if the school and the parents agree that the statement is necessary, what basis have the LEA for refusing an assessment when the school and the parents agree it is necessary?

(d) Has the LEA made a proper decision on the facts, or is it really relying on a policy, or applying the wrong provisions of the Code of Practice, such as saying that records have not been properly kept? This example means the LEA's decision does not relate to a proper consideration of the child's condition and the factual issues.

2. The refusal to reassess (section 172). Obviously, what is said about justifying a request for a reassessment with expert evidence earlier applies. The following issues may arise:

   (a) Has the child's condition changed?

   (b) Did the statement identify all the child's needs and make provision for all needs, or have new needs emerged?

   (c) Have matters become worse; if so, what is the effect?

   (d) What extra provision is necessary, or what alteration to provision is necessary?

   (e) Has the authority implemented efficiently the original statement?

3. The LEA's refusal to make a statement (section 169). Again the comments in relation to expert evidence and evidence from the school, or other relevant witnesses apply. The issues are likely to be as follows:

   (a) Has the assessment actually identified all the educational needs?

   (b) Has the assessment identified all the needs but failed to make provision for all the needs?

   (c) Can the school make provision for those needs, in fact and not in theory? Judgment of Harrison J, in *R -v- The Secretary of State for Education and Science ex parte W* supra is plainly relevant to this issue. There is a tendency in the Code of Practice and for local authorities to consider that school ought to make such provisions available, but the school itself is unable to do so.

   (d) Are the needs severe or complex?

   (e) Even if provision is available within the ordinary school, does the child require careful professional monitoring from the local education authority?

In general, the issues will be factual, taking into account the above questions. The issue is whether it is necessary to make a statement on the facts.

4. Appeals against statements of special educational needs (section 170) and in relation to amendments to statements, or refusals to amend after a reassessment. Again, the comments in relation to appropriate witnesses apply. The issues are likely to be as follows:

    (a) Does the statement in section 2 identify all the educational needs?

    (b) Does the statement in Part III make provision for all the educational needs?

    (c) Is some of the provision in Part V non-educational provision when it should be in Part III, and if there is a provision in Part V, ought there to be a similar provision specified in Part III, even if the Health Service is going to provide it, such as speech therapy or physiotherapy?

    (d) Can the provision be delivered in fact and not in theory?

    (e) Is the statement a proper description of the child as a whole child, and a proper attack on the problems?

    (f) Can the LEA show that the parents' choice of school should be rejected?

These questions apply whether or not this is an original statement, an amended statement, or an unaltered statement.

5. The decision to refuse to change the name of the school in the statement, para 8, schedule 10. The LEA can only refuse to insert parental preference if:

    (a) The school is unsuitable to the child's age, ability or aptitude and special educational needs; or

    (b) His attendance at the school would be incompatible with the provision of efficient education of children with whom he would be educated or efficient use of resources. These give rise to the following practical problems:

        (i) Can the child be successfully integrated into the ordinary school with the appropriate level of support?

        (ii) If this is disputed by the school why is that so?

(iii) What answer is there to the school's position, or has the school carefully considered the issue at all?

(iv) If the school is willing to attempt such integration, what is the basis for the LEA's opposition, and is the LEA in fact in breach of duties under other Acts such as the Chronically Sick and Disabled Persons Act, The Disabled Persons Services and Representation Act etc., i.e. to provide ramps and sufficient facilities and toilets for Disabled Persons?

(v) Does the child require speech therapy, physiotherapy or similar medically related provision, which is available in special schools but is not normally available in the ordinary school? If so, is the extent of this provision too much to be given either outside of school, and why can't a provision actually be given at an ordinary school?

6. A decision to cease to maintain a statement, paragraph 11, schedule 10. Again, what is said about calling appropriate expert evidence or witnesses applies.

(a) Can the child or young person survive without support which requires a statement and be expected to make reasonable progress?

(b) What is the real reason for the decision to cease to maintain a statement? Some LEAs simply have stopped at a certain age, although the young person needs support, and will continue to need support. A careful look at the decision and policy behind it should be carried out.

(c) In general, has the decision been made prematurely?

The essential question here is whether there is a good case for the withdrawal of the LEA or not.

Chapter 11

Practice and Procedure in the Tribunal

The new Tribunal has issued a User Friendly Booklet explaining to parents how they should appeal. The rules of procedure are intended to be designed to dispose of appeals fairly and quickly. As with the new assessment regulations, the tribunal aims to cut the delay that existed in many areas in the old system.

The procedure of the tribunal is governed by the Special Educational Needs Tribunal Regulations 1991 ST 1910. The rules of procedure are contained in the Regulations, see Appendix 6, pp.192–208.

The time limits are based on working days (Regulation 2) which are very sensibly defined. Working days do not include Saturdays, Sundays, bank holidays and the month of August. The following time limits apply:

1. Parents make an appeal. The appeal must be brought within two months of the decision (Regulation 7(3)). The tribunal office decides whether the tribunal can deal with the appeal; if they cannot do so the parents will be informed within ten days.

2. If they can deal with the appeal, the tribunal enters the appeal and sends the LEA a copy of the appeal. Details are also sent to the parent (Regulation 17(1)).

3. The LEA replies within 20 working days (Regulation 12(3)).

4. The tribunal office sends a copy of the LEA's reply to the parents; it also sends a form asking the parents for details of who they want to attend the hearing (Regulation 18).

5. The tribunal office sends copies to the parents or the LEA of any documents that the other party has sent (Regulation 17(4)).

6. Parents and the LEA return forms to the tribunal office.

7. The tribunal office informs the parties of the date and location of the hearing at least ten working days beforehand (Regulation 25(1)).

8. The tribunal office sends a written decision to the parents and the LEA within ten working days of the hearing (Regulation 31(5)).

MAKING AN APPEAL

A parent should fill in a Notice of Appeal, and send it to the Special Educational Needs Tribunal, Secretariat, The Exchange, 71 Victoria Street, London SW1. By Regulation 7 the notice should include the full name and address of the parents making the appeal; grounds of the appeal (which should include the decision or determination in relation to which the appeal is brought, or, if a statement, when the statement was first made); date; the name and address of the authority from whom the Notice was received or the statement was made; and the name, address and profession of any representative.

The form should be signed by the parent (Regulation 7(2)). The standard appeal form which is an appendix to this work indicates that more than very generalised reasons are expected by the tribunal. In other words, simply saying the statement does not meet the child's needs or make adequate provision would not be considered sufficient. As full details as it is possible to give of the appeal are required. It must be borne in mind that many parents will not have advice, and some of them may not be particularly literate, so it is to be hoped that the tribunal does not require too much in this regard. Sample grounds of appeal are set out on pp.148–9.

TIME

The appeal should be within two months of the decision by the tribunal office that the tribunal can deal with it (Regulation 7(3)). However (by Regulation 42), the tribunal has power to extend time for such further period as it considers reasonable in exceptional circumstances. These are not defined, but will depend on the facts of the case. Full details of exceptional circumstances must be given, in any application.

The parents can amend the appeal at any time before they are notified of the date of the hearing or can deliver a response to the LEA's reply to the ground of appeal (Regulation 8). Before a hearing the President may give leave (8(3)) or, at the hearing itself, the tribunal may give leave to amend the appeal or response (Regulation 8(3)B). Copies of all amendments or responses must be sent to the tribunal (Regulation 8). In the case of a response, 15 working days are specified (Regulation 8(2)).

WHAT DOCUMENTS SHOULD BE SENT TO THE TRIBUNAL

In addition to the Notice of Appeal, a copy of the LEA's letter giving a decision should be attached and, as already pointed out, a copy of the statement is mandatory under the Regulations. However, it would be wise to send all documents that are relevant to the type of appeal. Where a statement is under appeal, it should normally have attached to it all the parental representations and evidence, as well as the LEA's evidence and representations. A draft statement will not necessarily be included in this bundle; however, it may be useful and should normally be sent. Equally, copies of correspondence setting out particularly professional opinions on behalf of the authority which are not attached to the statement or important correspondence from the parents should also be sent. Any new expert report or information should be sent. Where parents have not been represented, this new evidence will often be crucial. If this new evidence is important in the appeal, the grounds of appeal should refer to it.

In relation to the other appeals, namely refusals against assess-ments, or refusals to accept parental choice of schools, the rules only require the actual decisions to be attached to the notice of appeal. However, there will often be correspondence in such cases, includ-ing those involving a refusal of a statement, or refusal to assess or reassess, where there should be in existence a number of reports, which should be sent in chronological order.

On receipt of the Notice of Appeal, the tribunal will first of all decide whether it can deal with the case (Regulation 17(2)). If it cannot, the parents will be informed. If it can, they will send copies of documents to the LEA. It must be remembered that the tribunal cannot deal with the following issues:

1. Delays by the LEA in carrying out an assessment, or the way in which it was carried out.

2. The way in which the provision is arranged by the LEA, or the fact that some of the provision is not being delivered by the LEA.

3. The way in which the school rather than the LEA is delivering provisions, or the fact that the school is not making some of the provision.

4. All non-educational needs and non-educational provision fall outside the statutory appeal. If, however, the parents believe that non-educational needs are in fact educational needs, it is for the tribunal to determine whether that is so or not. In practice, many non-educational needs are actually as much educational.

ACTION BY THE AUTHORITY ON RECEIPT OF NOTICE OF APPEAL

Regulation 12 provides for the LEA's duty to proceed. The LEA will have to reply within 20 working days of receiving copies of the notice of appeal form and the other documents Regulation 12(3). In their reply they must say whether or not they will oppose the appeal, and give a summary of their reasons (Regulation 12). A copy of their reply will be sent to the parents. If they decide not to oppose the appeal the tribunal will tell the parents whether they need to take any further action. If the appeal is opposed, the attendance form will be sent out to the parents to give details of who will attend the hearing.

Either side can seek directions (Regulation 19), which includes further particulars of any appeal or response (Regulation 21).

The LEA can, in exceptional cases, with the permission of the President at any time before the hearing, or with the permission of the tribunal itself, amend its reply or deliver a supplementary reply or amend a supplementary reply (Regulation 13(1)). However, so far as the LEA is concerned, it is to be noted that the President of the tribunal may give permission for such amendment on such terms as they think fit and this will include payment of costs or expenses. In the case of a parent (under Regulation 8), no such similar provision appears.

If the LEA does not reply within the time appointed by Regulation 12(3), or the authority states in writing that it does not resist the appeal or withdraws its opposition, the tribunal may determine the appeal on the basis of the Notice of Appeal without the hearing, or may, without notifying the authority, hold a hearing at which the authority is not represented (Regulation 15).

Regulation 42 allows an extension of time in exceptional circumstances. Statements by the President of the tribunal have indicated that, where an LEA fails to respond within the time limits, an extension will not be automatic. The use of the words 'exceptional circumstances' also indicates that the LEA, if seeking an extension of time, will have to set out in detail (as previously indicated), the circumstances upon which it relies. To qualify for exceptional circumstances some reason must be given *Savill -v- Southend H.A.* Times 28/12/94 Court of Appeal. Those reasons should in fact be set out in great detail.

NOTICE THAT THE APPEAL IS MISCONCEIVED

Regulation 14 provides for the authority to serve a notice on the tribunal to the effect that the appeal does not lie within the remit of, of cannot be entertained by the tribunal. Such notice, and the grounds for such contention, shall be served on the Secretary of the tribunal, and shall include an application of the appeal to be struck out. A copy is then sent to the appellant, and an application under this rule can be heard as a preliminary point of law or at the beginning of the hearing of the substantive appeal.

APPLICATION FOR DIRECTIONS

Regulation 19(4) provides for the parties to apply for directions. The application must be made in writing. The tribunal itself may at any time, of its own motion, as well as on the application of the parties, give such directions as are provided in the Regulation 19 in order to assist the tribunal to determine the issue.

Regulation 20 permits the tribunal to set aside directions notifying the party who applied. Regulation 21 provides for the President to give directions requiring particulars reasonably required to determine the appeal in either party's case. Regulation 22 provides for discovery, and inspection of documents. By Regulation 22(1) the President may give directions requiring a party to deliver to the tribunal any document or other material which the tribunal may require and which it is in the power of that party to deliver. Regulation 22(2) provides for discovery and inspection in such terms as may be granted by a county court.

By Regulation 23 the President may (by summons) require any person in England and Wales to attend as a witness at a hearing, at such time and place as may be specified in the summons. At the hearing that person will be required to answer any questions or produce documents or other material in his custody or under his control which relate to the matter in the appeal. The rule specifically limits this power in circumstances in which evidence can be given in a Court of law, where there is a need to protect intimate personal or financial circumstances and confidential information.

No person shall be required to attend unless he has been given at least five working days' notice or, if less than five days, he anyway accepts the notice. All necessary expenses must be paid to him.

In practice, the power to seek directions will be important in two ways. First, in relation to discovery, the appellant may well wish to see the county file or the school file if he believes that there is information on that file which has not been disclosed and which is of use in the case. It has been noticeable in judicial review proceedings that a great deal of important and additional material is contained in these files, which are not normally disclosed in the assessment. These are normally matters which would favour a child and his parents. It often includes correspondence from doctors or social services departments to the school and indicates that there is a medical condition being investigated, or provides information that is not made available to the parents. Initially, a request for discovery should be made to the local education authority. If it is not complied with, an application should be made for discovery.

So far as the issue of witness summons is concerned, often witnesses will be reluctant to attend, particularly if they work for schools or LEAs without such an order. In Industrial Tribunal the use of a witness summons has proved to be a means of obtaining evidence which is important to the case, when a witness is reluctant to attend because he or she is still working for an employer. Similarly, it is quite likely that in cases where teachers or other experts working for authorities can give useful evidence, they will not wish to be seen to be siding with any party, and would prefer actually to be summoned to attend the tribunal.

Finally, by Regulation 24 a failure to comply with directions will allow the tribunal to hear and determine the appeal without a hearing, dismiss it, or proceed without the party in default provided on discovery following directions.

THERE IS A LIMIT ON HOW MUCH MATERIAL CAN BE SENT

It must be borne in mind by the parents that, if they do obtain further evidence or reports, they cannot automatically expect to have them admitted, once the written part of the case is closed, and particularly once a hearing date is set. However, it must equally be borne in mind by all dealing with these matters that often when parents are unrepresented they do not easily have access to experts and additional advice. Where a parent is represented, and expert advice has been sought, solicitors who are applying for expert reports (whether on green form Legal Aid or in the normal course of preparation of the case) would be well advised to inform the tribunal if they are approaching these time limits, and to request an extension. Equally, experts consulted should remember that they ought to supply reports more quickly than some did in the past. The local authority's time to provide reports now is restricted; it is therefore not unreasonable to expect independent experts to provide reports within similar time constraints. Obviously, exceptions to this issue will normally be medical reports, and those reports could often be very important indeed, particularly if the local education authority has not sought sufficiently expert medical advice. In such cases there is no reason why an extension of time should not be sought in advance, it is important that these considerations are borne in mind.

THE HEARING

By Regulation 25, the Secretary for the tribunal shall with due regard to the convenience of the parties fix a time and place of the oral hearing, and not less than 10 days before the date fixed, shall send each party a notice that the hearing is to be at such a time and place. The 10 days can be shortened if the parties agree. Where the parties are intending to call busy experts, it is wise that they indicate available dates in advance to the Secretary of the tribunal.

The tribunal intends to bring those reasonably near to London to hearings in London. Where they consider that travelling is unreasonable, the tribunal intends to arrange a hearing at a convenient place near to the parties.

The Secretary of the tribunal shall include in or with the notice of the hearing the following information (by Regulation 25(2)):

(a) Information and guidance in the form approved by the President as to attendance of the hearing of parties and witnesses, the brining of documents and the right to representation or assistance by another person.

(b) A statement explaining the possible consequence of non-attendance and the right of an appellant and of the authority to be represented and for those who do not attend and are not represented to make representations in writing (Regulation 25(2)B).

The tribunal may alter the time and place of the hearing and give parties not less than five working days' notice of such alterations. Any altered date (unless the parties agree) shall not (unless the parties agree) be before the previously notified date. The tribunal has power to adjourn from time to time the oral hearing and if the time and place of the adjourned hearing is announced, no notice is required if it is done at the oral hearing (Regulation 25(5)).

Hearings are normally in private (Regulation 27). Public notice of the hearing is provided for, but the names of the appellant and the child concerned shall not be made public. The tribunal can, however, order a public hearing or the parties can agree one.

DETERMINATION OF THE APPEAL: THE POWER TO DETERMINE THE APPEAL WITHOUT A HEARING

By Regulation 26 the tribunal may:

(a) if the parties agree in writing; or

(b) in the circumstances prescribed in Regulation 15 and 24 where the LEA or parent do not in fact reply or comply with directions, determine the appeal or any particular issue without an oral hearing.

By Rule 24, if a party fails to attend when duly notified, the tribunal may:

(a) be satisfied that there is sufficient reason for the absence and adjourn the hearing; or

(b) If it is not satisfied there is sufficient reason for an absence, hear and determine the appeal and make such orders as to costs and expenses as it thinks fit.

Where a tribunal decides to dispose of an appeal in the absence of a party, due to a failure to attend, by Regulation 28 it must consider the representations in writing, submitted by that party, any response to a notice of a hearing, and all relevant documents including the notice of appeal.

Where an appellant has failed to attend or be represented at a hearing of which he was notified, and the tribunal has disposed of the appeal, no fresh appeal may be made by the appellant to the tribunal against the same disputed decision without the prior leave of the tribunal. However, the tribunal is able to review its decision under Regulation 33.

PROCEDURE AT THE HEARING

Regulation 29 applies to procedures at the hearing. According to the president of the tribunal, it is intended that, within the bounds of legal responsibilities, such hearings will be as informal as possible. The tribunal has powers to conduct the hearing in the manner it considers most suitable to the clarification of the issue before it and generally to the just handling of proceedings. It shall do so and, as far as it appears appropriate, seek to avoid formality in its proceedings (Rule 29(2)).

At the beginning of the hearing, it is intended that the Chairman will explain the order of proceedings which the tribunal proposes to adopt, and the parties shall be heard in such order as the tribunal shall determine. They shall be entitled to give evidence and call witnesses, to question any witnesses, and to address the tribunal, both on the evidence and generally on the subject matter of the appeal. The evidence before the tribunal may be given orally, or if the tribunal so orders, by affidavit or written statement.

THE NATURE OF THE EVIDENCE

As in industrial tribunals, the rules of evidence do not normally apply. The tribunal will give such weight to evidence which is not strictly admissible in an ordinary Court as it thinks fit. By Rule 30(3) it may receive evidence of any fact which appears to the tribunal to be relevant, and notwithstanding that such evidence would not be admissible in proceedings before a court of law. It shall not refuse to admit any evidence which is admissible or is relevant. At any hearing the tribunal may, if it is satisfied that it is just and reasonable to do so, permit a party to rely on grounds not stated in the notice of appeal, or as the case may be in any reply, and to adduce evidence not presented to the authority before or at the time it took the disputed decision. This is an entirely sensible rule, as parents will often discover important new evidence after a decision is made by a local authority. If they have not been represented and have relied on the authority's staff, it may be some considerable time afterwards, if they are not familiar with these issues, that they actually get important new evidence. Equally, the LEA may have new evidence, often due to a late change in the child's condition.

THE DECISION OF THE TRIBUNAL

Rule 31 requires that the decision shall be taken by a majority and it shall record whether the tribunal was unanimous or in the majority. If the tribunal comes down to only two members, the Chairman has the casting vote. The decision of the tribunal may be given orally at the end of the hearing or reversed. It must be recorded forthwith in a document, save in the case of a decision by consent which shall also contain or have annexed to it the statement of reasons in summary form of the decision, and each document or documents shall be signed by the Chairman (Regulation 31(2)).

The decision must also include the tribunal's notice of the right of appeal against the tribunal's decision. Where the decision is announced on the day of the hearing, that date is treated as the date of the decision (Regulation 31(5)).

By Regulation 32 the Tribunal has powers to review its decision on the application of any party or on its own motion if it is satisfied that:

(a) Its decision was wrongly made as a result of an error on the part of the tribunal's staff.

(b) A party was entitled to be hear at the hearing but failed to appear and be represented, had good and sufficient reason for failing to appeal.

(c) The interests of justice require.

In practice, it is likely that grounds (a) and (b) will occupy the tribunal on issues under Rule 32 and 32(c); is a wide rule. Where the application related to fresh evidence, it will have to be shown it was not available, because it was not known of or foreseen on the date of the hearing. It could, for example, include new expert evidence which shows the original diagnosis was negligent or wrong. Rule 32 appears to have been drafted on the basis of a wide discretion. It could include cases where the tribunal has been deliberately or inadequately misled by either party to the appeal, and an example of such an issue is that the evidence presented by an expert is discovered to be from a person who was not in fact an appropriate expert or appropriately qualified, although they improperly represented themselves as having such qualifications at the time of the hearing.

An application for a review may be made immediately following the decision at the hearing, or not later than ten working days after the date on which the decision was sent to the party. Such an application must be in writing, stating the grounds in full. If the tribunal proposes to review its decision of its own motion, it shall serve the notice of that proposal on the party within the same period (Rule 32(2)). Such an application can be refused by the President or the Chairman of the tribunal which decided the case, if in his opinion it has no reasonable prospect of success (Rule 32(3)). If it is not refused, under Rule 32(3) the parties shall have an opportunity to be heard on the application where a review shall be determined by the tribunal that decided the case or a new tribunal in these circumstances: where it is not reasonably practical for it to be heard by that tribunal; where a decision was made by the president acting alone under the rule. Having reviewed the decision, the president may set aside his decision under Rule 33. The Application is made in the same manner as applications under Rule 32.

COSTS AND EXPENSES

Rule 34 provides that the tribunal shall not normally make an order in respect of costs and expenses but may, subject to paragraph 2, make an order:

(a) Against a party (including an authority which has not submitted a written reply), and any party who has withdrawn his appeal or reply, if it is of the opinion that the party has acted frivolously or vexatiously, or that his conduct in making or pursuing or resisting an appeal was wholly unreasonable; and

(b) Against the authority where it considers the decision against which the appeal was brought was wholly unreasonable.

No such order shall be made unless the party has had an opportunity of making representations against the making of the order. An order for costs can be made as a specified sum made in connection of the whole or part of proceedings or costs to be taxed if not otherwise agreed (Rule 34(4)). If the costs are to be taxed, the tribunal has a power to direct the relevant scale under the county court rules (Regulation 34(5)).

In addition, the tribunal has power to transfer proceedings which can be more conveniently determined in another tribunal. This power may be important in cases where the family court is dealing with issues under the Children Act, which includes issues involving the assessment of children under the Children Act (Regulation 35).

GENERAL ISSUES AS TO THE CONDUCT OF THE HEARING

Mr. Trevor Aldridge Q.C., the President of the Tribunal has made it clear that the tribunal is attempting to proceed both quickly and informally, and seeks to avoid the problems of undue legality experienced in industrial tribunals. Either party has the right to be represented, and although it was hoped that LEAs would agree to a concordat that they would not use lawyers to represent them if the parents did not, the LEAs have not in fact agreed to this concordat. Bearing in mind that many parents with children with special needs, even if professionals, are under considerable strain, and many parents themselves have problems as many conditions are inherited, equally, dealing with children or a child with disabilities causes considerable emotional and physical strain both at home and in life in general, parents often find that if they can afford it, or obtain it, representation, whether by lawyers or by experienced charitable representatives, is of great assistance. It is, however, the view of the author, that this is a complex field involving complex issues of medical educational and many other factors. It is therefore advisable to use those experienced in the field, who have expertise, and the same applies to experts called by the parents or used by the parents or their representatives.

APPEALS

Appeals are on a point of law. Equally, it should be remembered that judicial review has still an important role to play. The issues of appeals, and the use of judicial review are considered in the next chapter.

GENERAL ISSUES AS TO THE CONDUCT OF THE CASE

For those representing parents and those acting for the local education authority, it is clearly important that the grounds of appeal or the supplemental statements to them identify the issues as clearly as possible. For the LEA, where the grounds of appeal have identified issues not addressed, these points need careful consideration.

As far as the hearing is concerned, the parties will normally be limited to two witnesses together with representation, assuming the parents are able to obtain representation (Regulation 30). The limitation on two witnesses is intended to mean two witnesses plus the parents, but for the LEA will mean that, in normal circumstances, they are limited to two witnesses. In practice, parents rarely bring more than one witness apart from themselves and normally that witness is an educational psychologist. However, in cases involving speech and language problems, it is normal to have, if it is at all possible, a speech and language therapist to give expert evidence on the child's difficulties and need for speech therapy, which is often a main area in dispute. In relation to cases involving integration, representatives of associations locally who are aware as to how integration has been achieved, particularly where adaptations are all that are required, can often give successful and important written reports. Rarely does a teacher or head teacher give evidence. This may change.

Where an interpreter is needed (this will obviously include not only those who speak a foreign language but those who need sign language), the tribunal will arrange for an interpreter to attend. It is to be noted that the tribunal will pay the expenses of those attending. This will include a fixed daily rate, which will contribute to or pay fees of expert witnesses.

If more than two witnesses are needed, then an application must be made in advance in writing and the tribunal Chairman will decide whether or not to grant the application (Regulation 30(1)). In some cases it may be necessary to have evidence from the school, or a teacher, as well as from a speech therapist and an educational psychologist. Equally, it is possible that there is a need for evidence on a medical issue. If solicitor and counsel are involved, Regulation 11(3) requires permission for both to attend.

CALLING THE CHILD OR YOUNG ADULT AS A WITNESS

The Code of Practice makes it clear that the wishes and views of the child should be sought and considered. With young adults, their views will often be quite crucial, but this does not necessarily mean it is advisable or good practice for a child or young adult to attend an appeal. Even if the hearing is an informal hearing and the tribunal will be informal, the young person may not find themselves in a position truly to express their views. Their views may be better expressed by their parents or in writing or even, if necessary, on a video. On some occasions it may be useful to have them attend; if so, it is not advisable for them to attend the full hearing. The wrong impression can well be given. There is an interesting story presently being told based on the truth. Under the old appeal system a parent brought their child who had great difficulty in concentrating to an appeal hearing. The child appeared to concentrate. Of course, the child was probably dreaming, but the wrong impression was given. It is likely that in cases involving young adults which determine their future up to the age of 19 years, particularly where they are mature and have strong views, the attendance of the young adult either at the hearing for part of the time or throughout the hearing would be advisable.

APPEALS WHICH INVOLVE THE ISSUES OF A NAMED SCHOOL

Paragraph 3 of Schedule 10 requires a local authority, where they make a statement in a case where the parent of a child has expressed a preference to a school, specify the name of the school unless:

(a) The school is unsuitable to the child's age, ability or aptitude of his special educational needs, or

(b) Attendance of the child at the school would be incompatible with the provision of efficient education for the children with whom he would be educated or the efficient use of resources.

Paragraph 8 of Schedule 10 allows the parent to request a change from the school named in the statement. This allows the parent to ask the local education authority to substitute the named grant-maintained, grant-maintained or maintained special school specified by the parent, where the request has been made at least 12 months after a previous request, the service of a final statement, an amended statement or, after the date of an appeal against the statement under section 170.

In these circumstances, the local education authority shall comply with the request unless the same conditions apply under section 3(3) as set out above.

In those circumstances the burden of proof is fairly and squarely on the LEA to show that the school is unsuitable, or that the child's attendance would be incompatible with the efficient education for children with whom he would be educated or the efficient use of resources.

Chapter 12

Appeals and Enforcement of Statutory Duties

An appeal lies from the Special Educational Tribunal by reasons of the provisions of section 181 of the Act. Section 181 amends the Tribunals and Enquiries Act 1992 so as to include the special educational needs Tribunals in the list of Tribunals coming under the direct supervision of the Council on Tribunals and to allow appeals from the Tribunal to the High Court on the point of law. Alternatively, the Tribunal may be required, by the rules of the Supreme Court, to state and sign a case for the opinion of the High Court.

As already pointed out in this work, the appeals given under the Act do not allow the Tribunal actually to police the enforcement of a statement, or the time limits under the regulations for assessments, review, or reassessment. Those issues remain issues outside of the jurisdiction of the Tribunal and are the province of the High Court on judicial review, or alternatively a complaint to the Minister under section 68 or 99 of the Education Act 1944. This remedy is less effective than a High Court application and there is no legal aid. Lastly there is a complaint to the Local Government Commissioner.

A complaint to the Local Government Commissioner is not appropriate in such circumstances as he can only comment on maladministration and rectify the effects of maladministration, possibly by suggesting some element of compensation. Such a complaint is not therefore appropriate for a case in which the authority is delaying, or does not in fact arrange the provision in the statement. As legal aid is available to the child directly and where an authority is either delaying, or failing to implement a statement, an application to the High Court for judicial review, which can be expedited and normally should be, is the appropriate means to proceed. The complaint to the Minister procedure actually takes longer, and as the Minister under such complaints does not in fact copy the correspondence to both sides, it has considerable room for error and mistakes. Such complaints take a long period of time, and could involve considerable costs to the parent in proving certain issues, whereas in judicial review legal aid is available to cover these issues.

Where the authority is in breach of the regulations, dealing with time limits, a complaint to the Minister could be a clumsy, time-consuming method to proceed in dealing with a plain breach of statutory duty.

APPEALS ON POINT OF LAW

It is important for those advising parents, and for parents who have conducted their own case or who have been assisted by charities and voluntary organisations, to be aware that legal aid is available to appeal the decision of the education appeal tribunal to the High Court. There is a limited time in which to appeal (some two months under the provisions of Order 55 of the Rules of the Supreme Court), although time can be extended, if good reason can be shown by the Rules of the Supreme Court. Legal aid is available and would be available to the child as well as to an appropriate parent under the Children Act reforms.

An appeal does not deal with factual issues; like judicial review it only deals with legal matters. Matters of law include such issues as failing to give adequate reasons. The Appeal Tribunal is bound to give adequate reasons for its decision, which include reasons which are sufficient to deal with the issues before and allow each party to know that the decision made actually deals with the issues before the Appeal Committee. These provisions were applied in Education Appeal Committees in special needs cases by the case of *R -v- Surrey Education Committee ex parte H 83 LGR* at pg. 219, the principles have been set out again clearly in *R -v- The Civil Service Appeal Board ex parte Cunningham* 1991 4 EAR pg. 310.

It is important to remember that factual issues are for the Appeal Committee, and that there is no jurisdiction on case stated or judicial review for the High Court to interfere so long as a decision is reached fairly and reasonably – see *R -v- Salford Education Authority ex parte L* 1994 Education Law Reports page 16.

There will no doubt be considerable scope for appeals relating to the rules of procedure, particularly those rules that allow the Appeal Tribunal to disqualify a party that delays from appearing further and in relation to its requirement as regards grounds of appeal, and admission of points for new evidence. It is, not however, the purpose of this work to anticipate what lawyers may or may not argue on behalf of parents. Obviously, there are a number of points of law which will arise on the construction of the new Act, particularly with regard, no doubt, to such matters as the meaning of the word 'necessary', and the provisions relating to choice of school.

In further editions of this work, this particular chapter is likely to expand considerably on these issues. The Code of Practice and its effect will no doubt also be a matter considered by the Higher Courts.

The parent's checklist

Questions to ask to indicate *suitability* of LEA mainstream school provision.

1. Preliminary Research

(a) Ask LEA for a copy of its policy on educating Spld children. If it hasn't one: why not?

(b) Every school is required to produce a prospectus: obtain and read the one for your named school. This gives an idea of ethos, background, aims and academic practice.

(c) Ask for copies of school's handouts and circulars to parent on special needs arrangements and provision.

(d) Who are the parent governors? Do they carry out their duty to see that statemented children are taught as outlined in the statement? Contact them and ask.

(e) How many schools like this does the LEA maintain? How special is it? What extra resources are available to it?

(f) From *Education Year Book*, or LEA statistics, ascertain size of school and number of teachers. Calculate average class size. Check this later from the head and by your own observation.

(g) Although Warnock suggests 20 per cent of school population at sometime have special needs, calculate $\frac{1}{10}$ of enrolment in suburban areas, $\frac{1}{7}$ of enrolment in inner city areas to have special needs. This indicates crudely the size of school's special educational needs problem. Note and relate to facts on resources and staffing gleaned on school visit.

2. Visit School

(a) *Talk to head:* What is attitude to special needs children? Supportive? Disinterested?

(b) What is attitude to Spld/dyslexia?

(c) What does *head* consider is the major problem faced by school's special needs staff?

(d) What is head's calculation of average size of class? (remember groups in excess of 20 will provide very difficult learning conditions for students with serious Spld).

(e) How many statemented children attend the school? How many with Spld?

(f) What is school's INSET policy for (i) class teachers (ii) special needs staff.

3. Enquire about national curriculum

(a) How broad? Flexibility is more important than breadth. Problems of implementation of national curriculum.

(b) What facilities are available for practical subjects work; art, craft, design etc?

(c) What is preferred teaching approach, if any? Formal, informal, multi sensory?

(d) What individual arrangements are made to help those weak in fundamentals?

(f) What arrangements can be made to make up teaching missed by late entry or Spld?

(g) Do students have regular access to typewriter, computer, word processor, tape recorder?

(h) Ask to see some standard text books for that age group. Calculate text difficulty using Fog index. Relate to student's reading ability. Wide discrepancy indicates degree of difficulty student will experience on curriculum.

4. Talk to head of Special Needs

(a) What is attitude to special needs children?

(b) What is attitude to Spld/dyslexia?

(c) What is major problem faced by special needs department? Check whether this is:

   (i) containing broadly based literacy difficulties in children from a range of backgrounds.

   (ii) teaching basic skills competence to slower learning students.

   (iii) dealing with social emotional and motivational problems.

   (iv) meeting individual special needs.

(d) Does the special needs department have its own accommodation, or does it use the classrooms of other departments, or other *ad hoc* arrangements.

(e) What resources and equipment are available?

(f) What structured multi-sensory programmes are used?

(g) If teaching is 'objectives' based,

   (i) how realistic are objectives?

(ii) how well do objectives integrate to make a coherent language programme which is different from what child has been given previously?

5. Visit a class *(try to go to one which contains a statemented pupil)*

(a) Check class size, note the sense of purpose or otherwise in the ongoing activity.

(b) Look at teaching methods. Try to assess the way in which information is presented. How much reading, note taking, copying, essay writing would be necessary for survival in that class?

(c) Note any special arrangements in operation for individual children.

(d) At end of lesson, try to talk briefly to class teacher. Was class teacher aware of the special needs of the statemented child? How sympathetic and knowledgeable is that class teacher towards the problems of the Spld/dyslexic student?

6. Summing Up

You should now be able to answer these key questions:

(a) How sympathetic are the staff?

(b) How knowledgeable and well trained in this special educational need?

(c) How suitable is the general curriculum?

(d) How detailed and individually appropriate is the special provision?

(e) How appropriate are the buildings and resources?

(f) Is this school conversant with the particular special needs of my child, can it make and maintain the required provision?

(g) Does this provision offered by LEA take due account of the efficient use of all resources, including my child?

(h) Will this provision result in fast gains, and good morale or slow gains, low curriculum success and falling morale.

(i) Can it competently meet my child's special educational needs?

Accept or reject the provision.

History notes written by Pearse, aged 8 years 0 months

WISC (R) Verbal Scale 136. Performance Scale 120
Dotting speed: R 30.2
L 31.4
Slow times show motor difficulty. Similar times
indicate ambidexterity.
Vernon Graded Word Spelling Test: score 7y 6m

The balll of Bucur hill
was sot by the Normins
and the sayes
won the balltl the Normims
hill becoos they Buculy
sayes becoos the truc the
ran att a way Normims
the sayes ran aul aster
som of
Normims but the
Normims koulld the
sayes
astur the that
them then ran
the
Normims killd the
of ohter sata sayens

Sample report

Name: **Date seen:**

Address: **Date of Birth:** 3 July
                                               Age: 11 years 4 months

Test Results

Ability

WISC(R) (Wechsler Intelligence Scale for Children (Revised))

Standard: verbal: average   *Ability :* Centile Rank = 80%
            visual: very high

                                               Full Scale IQ =   not quoted

Verbal Scale IQ =   96   *Performance Scale IQ =*   131

Information	6	Picture completion	12
Similarities	11	Picture arrangement	15
Arithmetic	9	Block design	18
Vocabulary	10	Object assembly	17
Comprehension	11	Coding	10
Digit span	(7)		

Average range 8–12: Individual scores vary from 1 to 19 for these tests.

Further Diagnostic Testing

Laterality
Handedness: for writing – Right. Dotting Speed: Right 21.2 seconds
                                                        Left   21.8 seconds

Fine motor control: slow, and close to ambidexterity

Eyedness:	Telescope:	Left	confusions &
	Aperture:	Middle & left, then right	uncertainties in
	Cone:	Right	binocular
			control

Left/right awareness:	confused

Memory

	WISC(R) Digit Span test	7 year 6 months
	British Ability Scales Recall of Digits Subtest	8 year 2 months. Centile 26. T44 below average auditory short term recall
	British Ability Scales Immediate Visual Recall	7 year 8 months. Centile 10. T37 Weak visual short term recall
	British Ability Scales Recall of Designs	9 year 8 months. Centile 28. T44 below average visuo-motor memory competence. Difficulties with orientation of designs on the page.

Abilities in:	*Difficulties in:*
Visual sequencing	Auditory short term recall
Visual perception	Fine motor control
Constructive visual thinking	

Attainment in Basic Skills

Reading
SINGLE WORD RECOGNITION

British Ability Scales Word Reading Test (A)	Reading age 7 years 3 months: Centile 4, T32 Very slow average response time of 4 secs per word. Accuracy rate 62% is low. Very weak word recognition skills

CONTINUOUS PROSE
Neale Analysis of Reading

	Reading accuracy:	Age 7 years 6 months
Ability (Form C)	Reading comprehension:	Age 8 years 5 months
	Reading speed 54 wpm	Age 8 years 5 months

Spelling
Vernon Graded Word Spelling Test Spelling age 6 years 8 months. Centile 2. Serious difficulties in spelling.

Writing Skill
Pen grip: angular right hand: page twisted through 90 degrees to write down to up

Fluency/speed: slow at 10 words per minute

Writing style: poorly controlled unjoined print script which lacks flexibility

Punctuation: omitted

Spelling: limited word choice and high error rate of 30%, indicate spelling difficulties

Sentence structure: adequate

Expression of ideas: restricted and immature

Tests of Number

British Ability Scales Basic Number Skills Test (C)	Number age 8 years 8 months: Centile 11. T38 Weak written calculation skills

Referral Details

was referred for assessment at chronological age 11 years 4 months by his parents, Mr and Mrs   .   has special educational needs requiring a special provision to be made. The   has produced a revised draft Statement on 18th September   Mr and Mrs   seek guidance on   's level of intellectual ability, his information processing competence in auditory and visual short term memory and fine motor skills, and his attainments in the basic curriculum skills of reading, spelling, writing and numeracy, so that they may be advised further on the nature and extent of   's difficulties in learning, and an appropriate provision which can be made for him in the school.

General Background

Prior to assessment, Mrs   confirmed that   had enjoyed a normal childhood, with developmental stages occurring at the expected time. No untreated difficulties remain in his vision or hearing which might restrict his literacy learning.   enjoys good health and does not take medication which might retard his learning competences.

The early development of his physical skills was normal, with the usual stages occurring as expected, culminating in the establishment of right hand preference, which appears to be somewhat inconsistent. The early development of speech was normal, with   making speech sounds accurately, and later expressing his ideas competently in words.

It is noted that   can be forgetful, and he experiences concentration and attention difficulties. His working memory skills will be investigated and commented on in this report.

shows signs of anxiety and stress, which appear to relate to his difficulties in learning. He has shown both temper tantrums and behavioural difficulties in school, and his sleep patterns are not particularly regular. Despite these signs of stress, he gets on effectively with other children outside the family, but has some difficulties with his brother at home and with older children in school. It is evident that   experiences difficulties in cognitive skills development and some social difficulty which will be investigated and commented on in this report.

General Level of Intellectual Ability

The Wechsler Intelligence Scale for Children (Form R) was administered to
This enables his problem solving to be assessed on two dimensions, the Verbal
using words and the Performance using hand and eye skills. On the Verbal scale,
had an IQ of 96 in the average ability range. In this section of the test, his subtest
scores fluctuated from the high side of average to below average. Score variations
like this are usually observed in the test profile of students with specific learning
difficulties.

Use of Language in Thinking

In the Verbal subtests, where direct application of speech to problem solving is
necessary,   achieved an average standard. In Similarities, where he had to use
abstract verbal reasoning skills to perceive the relationship between ideas, his
score is average. He achieved the same standard in Vocabulary, where he had to
define words in common English use, and also in Comprehension, where he had
to use receptive language skills to process complex speech about social situations.
scores on these three subtests confirm that he used speech adequately in verbal
problem solving.

Auditory Short Term Memory in Verbal Problem Solving

In Digit Span, which indicates the development of   's auditory short term
memory, his score of 7 is much below average and he shows marked difficulty in
this important information processing skill. He shows some limitation in auditory
short term memory capacity, and has poor ability to apply sequencing skills to
material held in short term memory.

In Arithmetic, where   had to use working memory skills to extract the sense
of the question and apply to it his knowledge of tables, his score of 9 is in the
average range. He achieved a lower standard in Information, where he had to
recall and use his general knowledge.

      's scores on these three subtests indicate that his ability to apply working
memory skills to verbal problem solving is limited.

Visual Thinking Competence

On the Performance Scale   had an IQ of 131, in the very high intellectual
category. In this section of the test, his subtest scores fluctuated from maximum
to average.

In Picture Completion, where   had to perceive the omissions in pictures, his
score of 12 is on the high side of average and he shows competent visual analysis.
In Picture Arrangement, where he had to place into a left to right order sets of
pictures which tell stories, his score of 15 is much above average and he shows
well developed visual sequencing skill.

In Block Design, where   had to build patterns using blocks, his score of 18 is
close to test maximum and he shows excellent visual perceptual skills. In Object
Assembly, where he had to build jigsaw puzzle type pictures from parts, his score
of 17 again approaches test maximum and he shows excellent constructive visual
thinking skill.

's scores on these subtests are at a very much above average standard, and indicate that this aspect of his problem solving is a considerable cognitive strength for him.

In Coding subtest, where   had to use visual short term memory and fine motor manipulation on a number coding task, his score of 10 is average. He shows some inefficiency in the application of both these skills to the copying process.

General Ability Level

It is undesirable to quote a full scale IQ score for   as this would conceal the disparity between his verbal problem solving which is average, and his visual problem solving which is in the very high intellectual category. He shows a pattern of high visual problem solving capability and average verbal problem solving capability with widely scattered test scores, the balance of which is adequately reflected by his above average ability centile ranking of 80.   's difficulties in learning require further investigation and comment in the next section of this report.

Further Diagnostic Testing

Tests of Laterality

HAND SKILLS
          writes with his right hand. On a test of dotting speed which enables a comparison to be made between the speed, accuracy and control of one hand with the other, he returned a right hand time of 21.2 seconds and a left hand time of 21.8 seconds for the test. These times are very similar and indicate that   is properly regarded as being ambidextrous. The times are some 6–8% slow and indicate that he has a degree of fine motor manipulative difficulty.

EYE SKILLS & SPATIAL AWARENESS
          shows quite marked uncertainty in monocular and binocular control skills, and these confusions and uncertainties were reflected by later inadequacies in his line tracking in reading.   is advised that the family doctor, Dr   should be asked to consider referring   to the Department of Ophthalmology at his local hospital, or to the Royal Berkshire Hospital, Reading, for administration of the Dunlop Test.

          's sense of left/right awareness is confused, and this adds to his difficulties in line tracking.

It is evident that   experiences fine motor and eye control difficulties which will have affects upon his attainments in literacy skills.

Tests of Memory

AUDITORY/VERBAL
          's score on the Digit Span subtest of WISC(R) was translated into an age score using the appropriate table on page 189 of the WISC manual. He achieved a 7 year 6 month level and shows marked retardations in auditory short term recall.

As a check on this, the British Ability Scales Recall of Digits Subtest was administered. On this test   achieved an 8 year 2 month level, on the 26th centile rank, and shows below average auditory short term recall. These results are consistent and indicate that   's auditory short term memory skills are below average.

VISUAL
The British Ability Scales Subtest of Immediate Visual Recall was administered. On this test,   achieved a 7 year 8 month level, on the 10th centile rank, and shows weak visual short term recall.

The British Ability Scales Recall of Designs Subtest was administered. On this test,   achieved a 9 year 8 month level, on the 28th centile rank, and shows below average visuo-motor memory competence.   shows particular difficulties with the orientation of designs on the page and was somewhat confused by his own habit of twisting the page when writing or drawing.

RESULTS ON COGNITIVE TESTS
On the tests of cognitive ability administered,   shows skills in learning in visual sequencing, visual perception, and constructive visual thinking. He shows difficulties in learning in auditory short term recall and fine motor skills which will lead to some limitations in his attainments in the basic curriculum skills.

Attainment in the Basic Skills

Reading

SINGLE WORD RECOGNITION
The British Ability Scales Word Reading Test A was administered. On this test, had to recognise and name single words presented out of context. He achieved a 7 year 3 month standard, on the 4th centile rank, and shows weak word recognition skills. He shows a very slow response time, at an average of 4 seconds per word. It is noted that his accuracy of word recognition is extremely low with a 62% accuracy level.   's word recognition skills are very weak.

CONTINUOUS PROSE
The Neale Analysis of Reading Ability (Form C) was administered. On this test had to read continuous passages of English prose of increasing difficulty; when reading accuracy, comprehension and speed are monitored. On word accuracy, he achieved a 7 year 6 month level, his comprehension was at an 8 year 5 month standard, and his reading speed at 54 words per minute was at a similar standard. These subtest scores confirm that   's continuous reading skills are inefficient.

Spelling

The Vernon Graded Word Spelling Test was administered. On this test,   had to write down words which were dictated. He achieved a 6 year 8 month standard, on the 2nd centile rank, and his spelling skills show very significant difficulty.

Writing

A test of   's continuous writing skill was administered and analysed. He holds his pen in an angular right hand grip, with the page twisted through 90 degrees, so that he writes from down to up rather than from left to right. His speed of writing production is slow at 10 words per minute.   uses a poorly controlled unjoined print script which lacks flexibility. In this work, punctuation marks are omitted and   appears not to understand basic punctuation rules. His spelling in writing is very weak, with a limited word choice being evident and an extremely high error rate of 30% indicating his serious spelling difficulties. 's sentence structure is adequate, but his expression of ideas in writing is limited and immature.

Tests of Number

The British Ability Scales Basic Number Skills Test (C) was administered. On this test   had to carry out simple addition, subtraction, multiplication, division, fractions and decimals calculations. He achieved an 8 year 8 month level, on the 11th centile rank, and his calculation skills are very weak.

Conclusions

On the tests of cognitive and literacy skills administered,   shows average verbal ability, very high visual ability, but has difficulties in learning in aspects of auditory and visual short term recall and fine motor control, which lead to restrictions and retardations in his reading, spelling, writing and numeracy, consistent with specific learning difficulty or dyslexia.

Personality

The CPQ Child Personality Questionnaire (Form A) by Catell and Porter was administered to   . This enables the personality of the student to be assessed on fourteen major dimensions.   's personality profile is attached as an appendix to this report. Key points in his profile are that   is reserved, lacks stability, is shy, shrewd and tense. Calculation of the optional second order factors in this test show him to be rather introverted, independent and anxious. It is therefore evident that   has quite marked behavioural difficulties which affect his personality to some extent, and these exceed those normally encountered in students with specific learning difficulties/dyslexia. Therefore,   's behavioural difficulties must be considered in the provision to be made for him, and should be written into his Statement as an area which contributes to his difficulties in learning.

Comments on the Statement of Special Educational Needs

Mr and Mrs   are advised that the Statement of Special Educational Needs produced by the   is lacking in some essential details which would enable an appropriate provision to be made for

In section 2, Special Educational Needs, no reference is made to   's quite marked difficulties in learning in aspects of auditory short term recall, visual short term recall and fine motor skills. It is agreed that the social/behavioural difficulties which   experiences have been mentioned, but the management of these difficulties is made much more difficult by the Authority's insistence that these needs should be met totally in the ordinary classroom of   local school.

The special educational provision does not refer to   's difficulties in memory and motor skills which are amenable to teaching and should have been included as part of the programme.   's literacy skills problems have been mentioned and some reference is made to developing competence in the establishment of better peer relationships, but this is going to be an unnecessarily complex task if it is attempted within the large classroom of the local school.

Educational Provision

The provision to be made for   should cover five major areas. In section one, his clearly evident difficulties in learning need to be addressed. One hour per week should be spent on the development of appropriate standards in fine motor control and working memory skills. The Somerset Thinking Skills Development Programme by Blagg, Ballinger and Gardiner, or the Instrumental Enrichment Programme by Professor Reuven Feuerstein will be relevant.

The second section of   's programme should deal with his obvious difficulties in literacy skills. He should be taught by means of a structured multi-sensory language programme, with *Dyslexia: A Language Training Course for Learners and Teachers* by Kathleen Hickey, being appropriate, as is *Alpha to Omega* by Hornsby and Shear, published by Heinemann, or the Lucy Cowdens Course available from Kingston Polytechnic.   requires some three hours per week on this work.

The third section of   's programme should address his difficulties in numeracy, with assistance being given to enable him to manipulate tables and number facts more accurately, and to handle the written aspects of numeracy much more efficiently. One hour per week should be given to this work.

The fourth section of   's programme should address his serious behaviour and personality difficulties, looking at his behavioural skills and improving these in the small group setting, so that he develops social competences which may be transferred into the larger class group.

The final section of   's programme should take account of his very marked curriculum skill deficiencies. Until these have been dealt with by appropriate specialist teaching, he will need some five hours support per week on the curriculum, to enable him to have access to the learning experiences provided in school.

Mr and Mrs   should note that the special provision to be made for   is detailed, and his local school may find it difficult to make and maintain the required provision.

They may find that independent specialist boarding schools can offer appropriate specialist support. It may be a more efficient use of the local Authority's resources to place   in a suitable specialist 'out county' school.

The Psychological Assessment Report

These matters should be considered in depth in the assessment report. The Institute's format is standard throughout the country and should be adhered to.

First page	test scores
Then page two and following:	Referred by parents, school/LEA/ other sources

Outline the student's abilities and problems leading to failure. Does family think child is clever? Is there a family incidence of similar in school work?

Background

1. *Early history – general milestones*

    Physical, visual, aural, speech development

2. *School history:*
    How fragmented? How helpful?

3. *Personal details:*
    Child's attitude, behavioural background. Concentration and attention, working memory competence. Is there an a priori emotional disturbance, or a consequent behavioural difficulty?

4. *Intellectual ability*
    Discuss subtests strengths WISC-R or BAS to highlight key abilities and difficulties in learning.

5. *Look at the extent and impact of the difficulties in learning*
    (a) Fine motor skills, left/right awareness, directions. Comment on motor skill development in relation to literacy.
    (b) Perception

Auditory:	Wepman
Visual:	Bender

    (c) Working memory skills

Tests	Testing
BAS	Immediate/delayed visual recall.

		Recall of digits. Recall of designs
or	Aston Index	Auditory & visual sequential memory
or	Benton	Appropriate subtests
or	Koppitz VADS	Oral/aural, oral written visual oral, visual written
or	ITPA	Auditory and visual sequential memory

Basic curriculum skills

6. Language skills

Speech, reading, spelling, writing, to comment in individual attainments in the basic curriculum skills to reach conclusion about effectiveness of student language skills when judged by the standards of others of this age, ability and background.

7. Assess numeracy skills

by British Ability Scales, Vernon/Gillham and Hesse if WISC-R arithmetic subtest score or parent/school reports suggest this is needed.

8. Personality and social skills

Using Eysenck Personality Questionnaire, or Child Personality Questionnaire by Cattell and Porter or 16PF by Cattell, looking particularly at sociability, dominance, impulsivity, sensitivity, insecurity, tension and anxiety, to relate the student's social and personality skills to the circumstances in which he learns, and consider the need to provide counselling and personality skills development as part of the student's programme.

9. Conclusion

Subject is of below/average/high/very high intellectual ability; has (marked) weaknesses in fine motor skills/working memory skills and behavioural/social/personality difficulty related to retardations in reading spelling, written language, and or numeracy. His difficulties are/are not in keeping with specific learning disability/dyslexia.

10. Teaching provisions

The range of teaching provisions to be made for students with specific learning difficulties will be wide and varied. The provision made must be individual and relate to the abilities and difficulties in learning experienced by the student. The provision should cover (a) learning skills, (b) (i) language skills, (ii) numeracy skills, (c) study/thinking skills, and (d) behavioural skills, and (e) link effectively to the school curriculum.

(a) learning skills

(i) Fine motor skill development (train the hand)

(ii) Laterality-sequencing training (where do I start?)

(iii) Working memory training: develop deliberate control of available capacity, extend capacity, teach discarding of irrelevant information, choose time for learning, switch modalities frequently, multi-sensory is best.

(iv) Visual perceptual training: skill in recongising shapes consistently.

(v) Auditory perceptual training: skill in recognising sounds consistently.

(b) (i) language skill

(vi) Language development through talk:
    (i) getting sounds and words right
    (ii) getting sentences right
    (iii) concept/idea/labelling
    (iv) creating an organisation for talk.

(vii) Structured multi-sensory training to develop simultaneous skills in reading, spelling and writing and making most effective use of deficient memory skills.

(b) (ii) numeracy skills

(viii) Number language training: using structured multi-sensory methods.

(c) study/thinking skills

(ix) Extraction, representation, storage and recall of ideas.

(x) Expression of ideas in writing.

(xi) Development of active control of the learning/thinking process in 'metacognition'.

(d) behavioural skills

Developing the competences to enable the learner to operate effectively in a range of social and learning groups with varying purposes, structures, climates.

11. Special educational needs

To be discussed – teaching help needed in some or all of the above.

(i) Specify extent of programme required (1) learning, (2) literacy, (3) numeracy, (4) social development, (5) curriculum support in terms of hours per week.

(ii) If exam concessions certificate appropriate, please issue.

(iii) Refer parents to headteacher or remedial advisor for help. Advise on rights under Education ACT 1981, if necessary.

(iv) If in independent sector, the schools listed in Appendix 5 can help. Fees range from £8,000 to £12,000+. It is unlikely that LEAs or charities will pay.

Notice of Appeal

Notice of Appeal to the Special Educational Needs Tribunal

Please use this form if you want to send a notice of appeal to the Special Educational Needs Tribunal. You must send in this form within two months of receiving the Local Educational Authority's decision that you are appealing against. If the end of the two month period falls in August, you will have until 1 September to make your appeal.

Please fill in the boxes below. This form has to be photocopied, so please use black ink and capital letters.

Section 1

Please give below the details of the child, for whom the appeal is being made:

Child's surname ....

Child's first names ....

Child's date of birth ....

Child's gender M/F ....

It will help us if you tick one of the boxes below. You do not have to, but the information will give the tribunal useful statistics. All information is kept in the strictest confidence. The tribunal is registered under the Data Protection Act.

Child's ethnic origin:

☐ Black African   ☐ Bangladeshi   ☐ Chinese

☐ Black Caribbean   ☐ Indian   ☐ White

☐ Black Other*   ☐ Pakistani   ☐ Other*

* If you have ticked other, please give details:...................................

....

....

Section 2

Please give your details as follows:

☐ Mr ☐ Mrs ☐ Miss ☐ Ms ☐ Other

Your surname ....

First names...

Your relationship to the child ....

....

eg parent, guardian, etc

Your address ....

....

....

.... Postcode ....

Your telephone number, if any...

Section 3

If you want tribunal papers to be sent to another person who will be representing you, please give the following details:

Representative's name

....

Representative's address ....

....

....

.... Postcode ....

Representative's telephone

number, if any: ....

Representative's profession

....

Will the representative be attending the tribunal (either with you or instead of you)?

☐ Yes ☐ No ☐ Not sure

Section 4

Please give the name of the local education authority whose decision you are appealing against:

....

Please give the date you received the decision:

....

Please give the reasons for your appeal:

....

....

....

....

....

....

....

....

....

....

....

....

....

....

....

....

....

....

Section 5

If you live in Wales, do you want the hearing to be in Welsh?

☐ Yes ☐ No

Section 6

Please make sure you send the following documents with this appeal form:

- a copy of your child's statement of special educational needs (if he/she has one);

- any other documents attached to the statement (appendices);

- a copy of the letter (notice) from the LEA which sets out the decision against which you are appealing;

You will be able to send further documents at a later date if you want.

Your signature...

Date ....

Please return this form together with any supporting documents to the address below:

Special Educational Needs Tribunal
71 Victoria Street
LONDON SW1
Telephone: 0171 925 6925

GROUNDS OF APPEAL

1. Special Educational Needs – Part II

The Statement is deficient in failing to identify all of Daniel's special educational needs and it is in particular not lawful or appropriate to describe Daniel's special educational needs as being 'described in detail in the attached Appendices'. The Statement must set out in detail the child's needs which are in particular:

   (i) Daniel is of average verbal ability and high visual ability.

   (ii) Daniel has severe specific learning difficulties.

   (iii) Daniel has severe difficulties with spelling skills – he is currently some 3½ years behind his chronological age.

   (iv) Daniel has difficulties in auditory and visual short term memory skills – not recognised in Statement.

   (v) Daniel has difficulties with fine motor control skills – not recognised in Statement.

   (vi) Daniel has difficulties with reading skills particularly reading accuracy, comprehension and speed – in reading accuracy he is functioning nearly 5 years behind his chronological age.

   (vii) Daniel has difficulties with number skills – oral calculation skills in particular are weak.

   (viii) Daniel has a need for help in the development of skills in learning.

   (ix) Daniel has a need for in-class support to enable him to access the Curriculum.

2. Special Educational Provision

   (A) In failing to identify all of Daniel's educational needs the Education Authority has failed in its duty so to do and failed to comply with the guidelines laid down in the Code of Practice and the Law as contained in the decision of the Court of Appeal in *R -v- Secretary of State for Education and Science Ex Parte E.* If the needs are not correctly identified the provision to meet the needs cannot be appropriate.

   (B) The Statement does not set out which needs will be met by the school and which will be met by the Education Authority as it is required to do so by Law.

   (C) Overall the Provision Section in the Statement is vague and non specific and contains little of substance. In addition it does not comply with Regulation 13 of the Education (Special Educational Needs) Regulations.

   (D) Daniel requires a very detailed and specialist provision as follows:

      (i) Learning skills – to help with the development of motor and memory skills Daniel needs to follow a course such as the Instrumental Enrichment Programme by Professor Reuven Feuerstein or the Somerset Thinking Skills Development Course by Blague and Ballinger – 2 hours per week arranged in short frequent daily sessions spread evenly over the week.

(ii) Daniel should follow a structured multi-sensory language programme such as 'The Dyslexia Institute Skills Development Programme – Literacy', 'Alpha to Omega' by Hornsby and Shear or 'Dyslexia: A Training Course for Learners and Teachers' by Kathleen Hickey – 5 hours per week targeted skill based teaching required with the lessons being arranged in short frequent daily sessions spread evenly over the week.

(iii) Number skills – to help Daniel in difficulties with his oral calculation skills and to help him develop additional competencies in number skills he requires 1 hour per week structured multi-sensory teaching.

(iv) The provision required for Daniel should be delivered by a teacher who has the appropriate specialist qualifications in teaching children with specific learning difficulties such as the RSA or BDA Diploma, and should be delivered on a 1:1 basis or in small group (no more than 2/3 pupils) situations.

(v) If Daniel is to be placed in a mainstream school he will require a further 5 hours in-class support to enable him to access the Curriculum.

(vi) In all the provision required for Daniel is in excess of 8 hours per week specialist teaching and 5 hours in-class support. It is very detailed and specialised and requires a considerable in-put over the week. The Education Authority would find it very difficult for this type of provision to be delivered effectively in a mainstream school. In addition Daniel would find it very difficult to cope with the National Curriculum.

(vii) In view of the impracticability both for Daniel and the Education Authority in coping with such a programme in a mainstream school a more appropriate placement and a more efficient use of resources would be for the Local Education Authority to place Daniel in a residential school for children with specific learning difficulties providing small teaching groups, individual specialist teaching and a modified specialist Curriculum such as Northease Manor, where his educational, emotional and social needs can continue to be met throughout the day in a carefully structured and caring environment.

(viii) Finally, it is to be noted that in Section IV of the Statement the Education Authority have not actually named a school.

1993 Education Act

CHILDREN WITH SPECIAL EDUCATIONAL NEEDS

Introductory

156.–(1) For the purposes of the Education Acts, a child has 'special educational needs' if he has a learning difficulty which calls for special educational provision to be made for him.

(2) For the purposes of this Act, subject to subsection (3) below, a child has a 'learning difficulty' if–

(a) he has a significantly greater difficulty in learning than the majority of children of his age,

(b) he has a disability which either prevents or hinders him from making use of educational facilities of a kind generally provided for children of his age in schools within the area of the local education authority, or

(c) he is under the age of five years and is, or would be if special educational provision were not made for him, likely to fall within paragraph (a) or (b) when over that age.

(3) A child is not to be taken as having a learning difficulty solely because the language (or form of the language) in which he is, or will be, taught is different from a language (or form of a language) which has at any time been spoken in his home.

(4) In the Education Acts, 'special educational provision' means–

(a) in relation to a child who has attained the age of two years, educational provision which is additional to, or otherwise different from, the educational provision made generally for children of his age in schools maintained by the local education authority (other than special schools) or grant-maintained schools in their area, and

(b) in relation to a child under that age, educational provision of any kind.

(5) In this Part of this Act, 'child' includes any person who has not attained the age of nineteen years and is a registered pupil at a school.

Code of practice

157.–(1) The Secretary of State shall issue, and may from time to time revise, a code of practice giving practical guidance in respect of the discharge by local education authorities and the governing bodies of maintained or grant-maintained schools, or grant-maintained special schools, of their functions under this Part of this Act.

(2) It shall be the duty of–

(a) local education authorities, and such governing bodies, exercising functions under this Part of this Act, and

(b) any other person exercising any function for the purpose of the discharge by local education authorities, and such governing bodies, of functions under this Part of this Act,

to have regard to the provisions of the code.

(3) On any appeal, the Tribunal shall have regard to any provision of the code which appears to the Tribunal to be relevant to any question arising on the appeal.

(4) The Secretary of State shall publish the code as for the time being in force.

158.–(1) Where the Secretary of State proposes to issue or revise a code of practice, he shall prepare a draft of the code (or revised code).

(2) The Secretary of State shall consult such persons about the draft as he thinks fit and shall consider any representations made by them.

(3) If he determines to proceed with the draft (either in its original form or with such modifications as he thinks fit) he shall lay it before both Houses of Parliament.

(4) If the draft is approved by resolution of each House, the Secretary of State shall issue the code in the form of the draft and the code shall come into effect on such day as the Secretary of State may by order appoint.

Special educational provision: general

159. A local education authority shall keep under review the arrangements made by them for special educational provision and, in doing so, shall, to the extent that it appears necessary or desirable for the purpose of co-ordinating provision for children with special educational needs, consult the funding authority and the governing bodies of county, voluntary, maintained special and grant-maintained schools in their area.

160.–(1) Any person exercising any functions under this Part of this Act in respect of a child with special educational needs who should be educated in a school shall secure that, if the conditions mentioned in subsection (2) below are satisfied, the child is educated in a school which is not a special school unless that is incompatible with the wishes of his parent.

(2) The conditions are that educating the child in a school which is not a special school is compatible with–

(a) his receiving the special educational provision which his learning difficulty calls for,

(b) the provision of efficient education for the children with whom he will be educated, and

(c) the efficient use of resources.

161.–(1) The governing body, in the case of a county, voluntary or grant-maintained school, and the local education authority, in the case of a maintained nursery school, shall–

(a) use their best endeavours, in exercising their functions in relation to the school, to secure that if any registered pupil has special educational needs the special educational provision which his learning difficulty calls for is made,

(b) secure that, where the responsible person has been informed by the local education authority that a registered pupils has special educational needs, those needs are made known to all who are likely to teach him, and

(c) secure that the teachers in the school are aware of the importance of identifying, and providing for, those registered pupils who have special educational needs.

(2) In subsection (1)(b) above, 'the responsible person' means–

(a) in the case of a county, voluntary or grant-maintained school, the head teacher or the appropriate governor (that is, the chairman of the governing body or, where the governing body have designated another governor for the purposes of this paragraph, that other governor), and

(b) in the case of a nursery school, the head teacher.

(3) To the extent that it appears necessary or desirable for the purpose of co-ordinating provision for children with special educational needs–

(a) the governing bodies of county, voluntary and grant-maintained schools shall, in exercising functions relating to the provision for such children, consult the local education authority, the funding authority and the governing bodies of other such schools, and

(b) in relation to maintained nursery schools, the local education authority shall, in exercising those functions, consult the funding authority and the governing bodies of county, voluntary and grant-maintained schools.

(4) Where a child who has special educational needs is being educated in a county, voluntary or grant-maintained school or a maintained nursery school, those concerned with making special educational provision for the child shall secure, so far as is reasonably practicable and is compatible with–

(a) the child receiving the special educational provision which his learning difficulty calls for,

(b) the provision of efficient education for the children with whom he will be educated, and

(c) the efficient use of resources,

that the child engages in the activities of the school together with children who do not have special educational needs.

(5) The annual report for each county, voluntary, maintained special or grant-maintained school shall include a report containing such information as may be prescribed about the implementation of the governing body's policy for pupils with special educational needs; and in this subsection 'annual report' means the report prepared under the articles of government

for the school in accordance with section 30 of the Education (No. 2) Act 1986 or, as the case may be, paragraph 8 of Schedule 6 to this Act.

162.–(1) A local education authority may for the purpose only of assisting–

(a) the governing bodies of county, voluntary or grant-maintained school in their or any other area in the performance of the governing bodies' duties under section 161(1)(a) of this Act, or

(b) the governing bodies of maintained or grant-maintained special schools in their or any other area in the performance of the governing bodies' duties,

supply goods or services to them.

(2) The terms on which goods or services are supplied by local education authorities to the governing bodies of grant-maintained schools or grant-maintained special schools, or to the governing bodies of county, voluntary or maintained special schools in any other area, under this section may, in such circumstances as may be prescribed, include such terms as to payment as may be prescribed.

(3) This section is without prejudice to the generality of any other power of local education authorities to supply goods or services.

163.–(1) Where a local education authority are satisfied that it would be inappropriate for the special educational provision (or any part of the special educational provision) which a learning difficulty of a child in their area calls for to be made in a school, they may arrange for the provision (or, as the case may be, for that part of it) to be made otherwise than in a school.

(2) Before making an arrangement under this section, a local education authority shall consult the child's parent.

164.–(1) A local education authority may make such arrangements as they think fit to enable a child for whom they maintain a statement under section 168 of this Act to attend an institution outside England and Wales which specialises in providing for children with special needs.

(2) In subsection (1) above, 'children with special needs' means children who have particular needs which would be special educational needs if those children were in England and Wales.

(3) Where a local education authority make arrangements under this section in respect of a child, those arrangements may in particular include contributing to or paying–

(a) fees charged by the institution,

(b) expenses reasonably incurred in maintaining him while he is at the institution or travelling to or from it,

(c) his travelling expenses, and

(d) expenses reasonably incurred by any person accompanying him while he is travelling or staying at the institution.

(4) this section is without prejudice to any other powers of a local education authority.

Identification and assessment of children with special educational needs

165.–(1) A local education authority shall exercise their powers with a view to securing that, of the children for whom they are responsible, they identify those to whom subsection (2) below applies.

(2) This subsection applies to a child if–

(a) he has special educational needs, and

(b) it is necessary for the authority to determine the special educational provision which any learning difficulty he may have calls for.

(3) For the purposes of this Part of this Act, a local education authority are responsible for a child if he is in their area and–

(a) he is a registered pupil at a maintained, grant-maintained or grant-maintained special school,

(b) education is provided for him at a school which is not a maintained, grant-maintained or grant-maintained special school at the expense of the authority or the funding authority,

(c) he does not come within paragraph (a) or (b) above but is a registered pupil at a school and has been brought to the authority's attention as having (or probably having) special educational needs, or

(d) he is not a registered pupil at a school, is not under the age of two years or over compulsory school age and has been brought to their attention as having (or probably having) special educational needs.

166.–(1) Where it appears to a local education authority that any District Health Authority or local authority could, by taking any specified action, help in the exercise of any of their functions under this Part of this Act, they may request the help of the authority, specifying the action in question.

(2) An authority whose help is so requested shall comply with the request unless–

(a) they consider that the help requested is not necessary for the purpose of the exercise by the local education authority of those functions, or

(b) subsection (3) below applies.

(3) this subsection applies–

(a) in the case of a District Health Authority, if that authority consider that, having regard to the resources available to them for the purpose of the exercise of their functions under the National Health Service Act 1977, it is not reasonable for them to comply with the request, or

(b) in the case of a local authority, if that authority consider that the request is not compatible with their own statutory or other duties and obligations or unduly prejudices the discharge of any of their functions.

(4) Regulations may provide that, where an authority are under a duty by virtue of subsection (2) above to comply with a request to help a local education authority in the making of an assessment under section 167 of this Act or a statement under section 168 of this Act, they must, subject to prescribed exceptions, comply with the request within the prescribed period.

(5) In this section, 'local authority' means a county council, a metropolitan district council, a London borough council or the Common Council of the City of London.

167.–(1) Where a local education authority are of the opinion that a child for whom they are responsible falls, or probably falls, within subsection (2) below, they shall serve a notice on the child's parent informing him–

(a) that they propose to make an assessment of the child's educational needs,

(b) of the procedure to be followed in making the assessment,

(c) of the name of the officer of the authority from whom further information may be obtained, and

(d) of the parent's right to make representations, and submit written evidence, to the authority within such period (which shall not be less than twenty-nine days beginning with the date on which the notice is served) as may be specified in the notice.

(2) A child falls within this subsection if–

(a) he has special educational needs, and

(b) it is necessary for the authority to determine the special educational provision which any learning difficulty he may have calls for.

(3) Where–

(a) a local education authority have served a notice under subsection (1) above and the period specified in the notice in accordance with subsection (1)(d) above has expired, and

(b) the authority remain of the opinion, after taking into account any representations made and any evidence submitted to them in response to the notice, that the child falls, or probably falls, within subsection (2) above,

they shall make an assessment of his educational needs.

(4) Where a local education authority decide to make an assessment under this section, they shall give notice in writing to the child's parent of that decision and of their reasons for making it.

(5) Schedule 9 to this Act (which makes provision in relation to the making of assessments under this section) shall have effect.

(6) Where, at any time after serving a notice under subsection (1) above, a local education authority decide not to assess the educational needs of the child concerned they shall give notice in writing to the child's parent of their decision.

168.–(1) If, in the light of an assessment under section 167 of this Act of any child's educational needs and of any representations made by the child's parent in pursuance of Schedule 10 to this Act, it is necessary for the local education authority to determine the special educational provision which any learning difficulty he may have calls for, the authority shall make and maintain a statement of his special educational needs.

(2) The statement shall be in such form and contain such information as may be prescribed.

(3) In particular, the statement shall–

(a) give details of the authority's assessment of the child's special educational needs, and

(b) specify the special educational provision to be made for the purpose of meeting those needs, including the particulars required by subsection (4) below.

(4) The statement shall–

(a) specify the type of school or other institution which the local education authority consider would be appropriate for the child,

(b) if they are not required under Schedule 10 to this Act to specify the name of any school in the statement, specify the name of any school or institution (whether in the United Kingdom or elsewhere) which they consider would be appropriate for the child and should be specified in the statement, and

(c) specify any provision for the child for which they make arrangements under section 163 of this Act and which they consider should be specified in the statement.

(5) Where a local education authority maintain a statement under this section–

(a) unless the child's parent has made suitable arrangements, the authority–

(i) shall arrange that the special educational provision specified in the statement is made for the child, and

(ii) may arrange that any non-educational provision specified in the statement is made for him in such manner as they consider appropriate, and

(b) if the name of a maintained, grant-maintained or grant-maintained special school is specified in the statement, the governing body of the school shall admit the child to the school.

(6) Subsection (5)(b) above does not affect any power to exclude from a school a pupil who is already a registered pupil there.

(7) Schedule 10 to this Act (which makes provision in relation to the making and maintenance of statements under this section) shall have effect.

169.–(1) If, after making an assessment under section 167 of this Act of the educational needs of any child for whom no statement is maintained under section 168 of this Act, the local education authority do not propose to make such a statement, they shall give notice in writing of their decision, and of the effect of subsection (2) below, to the child's parent.

(2) In such a case, the child's parent may appeal to the Tribunal against the decision.

(3) On an appeal under this section, the Tribunal may–

(a) dismiss the appeal,

(b) order the local education authority to make and maintain such a statement, or

(c) remit the case to the authority for them to reconsider whether, having regard to any observations made by the Tribunal, it is necessary for the authority to determine the special educational provision which any learning difficulty the child may have calls for.

170.–(1) The parent of a child for whom a local education authority maintain a statement under section 168 of this Act may–

(a) when the statement is first made,

(b) where the description in the statement of the authority's assessment of the child's special educational needs, or the special educational provision specified in the statement, is amended, or

(c) where, after conducting an assessment of the educational needs of the child under section 167 of this Act, the local education authority determine not to amend the statement,

appeal to the Tribunal against the description in the statement of the authority's assessment of the child's special educational needs, the special educational provision specified in the statement or, if no school is named in the statement, that fact.

(2) Subsection (1)(b) above does not apply where the amendment is made in pursuance of paragraph 8 or 11(3)(b) of Schedule 10 to this Act or directions under section 197 of this Act; and subsection (1)(c) above does not apply to a determination made following the service of notice under paragraph 10 of Schedule 10 to this Act of a proposal to amend the statement.

(3) On an appeal under this section, the Tribunal may–

(a) dismiss the appeal,

(b) order the authority to amend the statement, so far as it describes the authority's assessment of the child's special educational needs or specifies the special educational provision, and make such other consequential amendments to the statement as the Tribunal think fit, or

(c) order the authority to cease to maintain the statement.

(4) On an appeal under this section the Tribunal shall not order the local education authority to specify the name of any school in the statement (either in substitution for an existing name or in a case where no school is named) unless–

(a) the parent has expressed a preference for the school in pursuance of arrangements under paragraph 3 of Schedule 10 to this Act, or

(b) in the proceedings the parent, the local education authority or both have proposed the school.

(5) Before determining any appeal under this section the Tribunal may, with the agreement of the parties, correct any deficiency in the statement.

171.–(1) This section applies where–

(a) a local education authority maintain a statement for a child under section 168 of this Act, and

(b) in pursuance of the statement education is provided for the child at–

(i) a school maintained by another local education authority,

(ii) a grant-maintained school, or

(iii) a grant-maintained special school.

(2) Any person authorised by the local education authority shall be entitled to have access at any reasonable time to the premises of any such school for the purpose of monitoring the special educational provision made in pursuance of the statement for the child at the school.

172.–(1) Regulations may prescribe the frequency with which assessments under section 167 of this Act are to be repeated in respect of children for whom statements are maintained under section 168 of this Act.

(2) Where–

(a) the parent of a child for whom a statement is maintained under section 168 of this Act asks the local education authority to arrange for an assessment to be made in respect of the child under section 167 of this Act,

(b) such an assessment has not been made within the period of six months ending with the date on which the request is made, and

(c) it is necessary for the authority to make a further assessment under that section,

the authority shall comply with the request.

(3) If in any case where subsection (2)(a) and (b) above applies the authority determine not to comply with the request–

(a) they shall give notice of that fact and of the effect of paragraph (b) below to the child's parent, and

(b) the parent may appeal to the Tribunal against the determination.

(4) On an appeal under subsection (3) above, the Tribunal may–

(a) dismiss the appeal, or

(b) order the authority to arrange for an assessment to be made in respect of the child under section 167 of this Act.

(5) A statement under section 168 of this Act shall be reviewed by the local education authority–

(a) on the making of an assessment in respect of the child concerned under section 167 of this Act, and

(b) in any event, within the period of twelve months beginning with the making of the statement or, as the case may be, with the previous review.

(6) Regulations may make provision–

(a) as to the manner in which reviews of such statements are to be conducted,

(b) as to the participation in such reviews of such persons as may be prescribed, and

(c) in connection with such other matters relating to such reviews as the Secretary of State considers appropriate.

173.–(1) Where–

(a) the parent of a child for whom a local education authority are responsible but for whom no statement is maintained under section 168 of this Act asks the authority to arrange for an assessment to be made in respect of the child under section 167 of this Act,

(b) such an assessment has not been made within the period of six months ending with the date on which the request is made, and

(c) it is necessary for the authority to make an assessment under that section,

the authority shall comply with the request.

(2) If in any case where subsection (1)(a) and (b) above applies the authority determine not to comply with the request–

(a) they shall give notice of that fact and of the effect of paragraph (b) below to the child's parent, and

(b) the parent may appeal to the Tribunal against the determination.

(3) On an appeal under subsection (2) above the Tribunal may–

(a) dismiss the appeal, or

(b) order the authority to arrange for an assessment to be made in respect of the child under section 167 of this Act.

174.–(1) Where in the case of a child for whom a local education authority are responsible but for whom no statement is maintained under section 168 of this Act–

(a) a grant-maintained school is specified in a direction in respect of the child under section 13 of this Act,

(b) the governing body of the school ask the authority to arrange for an assessment to be made in respect of the child under section 167 of this Act, and

(c) such an assessment has not been made within the period of six months ending with the date on which the request is made,

the local education authority shall serve a notice under subsection (2) below on the child's parent.

(2) The notice shall inform the child's parent–

(a) that the local education authority propose to make an assessment of the child's educational needs,

(b) of the procedure to be followed in making the assessment,

(c) of the name of the officer of the authority from whom further information may be obtained, and

(d) of the parent's right to make representations, and submit written evidence, to the authority within such period (which shall not be less than twenty-nine days beginning with the date on which the notice is served) as may be specified in the notice.

(3) Where–

(a) a local education authority have served a notice under subsection (2) above and the period specified in the notice in accordance with subsection (2)(d) above has expired, and

(b) the authority are of the opinion, after taking into account any representations made and any evidence submitted to them in response to the notice, that the child falls, or probably falls, within subsection (4) below,

they shall make an assessment of his educational needs under section 167 of this Act.

(4) A child falls within this subsection if–

(a) he has special educational needs, and

(b) it is necessary to determine the special educational provision which any learning difficulty he may have calls for.

(5) Where a local education authority decide in pursuance of this section to make an assessment under that section, they shall give notice in writing to the child's parent, and to the governing body of the grant-maintained school, of that decision and of their reasons for making it.

(6) where, at any time after serving a notice under subsection (2) above, a local education authority decide not to assess the educational needs of the child concerned, they shall give notice in writing to the child's parent and to the governing body of the grant-maintained school of their decision.

175.–(1) Where a local education authority are of the opinion that a child in their area who is under the age of two years falls, or probably falls, within subsection (2) below–

(a) they may, with the consent of his parent, make an assessment of the child's educational needs, and

(b) they shall make such an assessment at the request of his parent.

(2) A child falls within this subsection if–

(a) he has special educational needs, and

(b) it is necessary for the authority to determine the special educational provision which any learning difficulty he may have calls for.

(3) An assessment under this section shall be made in such manner as the authority consider appropriate.

(4) After making an assessment under this section, the authority–

(a) may make a statement of the child's special educational needs, and

(b) may maintain that statement,

in such manner as they consider appropriate.

176.–(1) This section applies where a District Health Authority or a National Health Service trust, in the course of exercising any of their functions in relation to a child who is under the age of five years, form the opinion that he has (or probably has) special educational needs.

(2) The health authority or trust shall–

    (a) inform the child's parent of their opinion and of their duty under this section, and

    (b) after giving the parent an opportunity to discuss that opinion with an officer of the health authority or trust, bring it to the attention of the appropriate local educational authority.

(3) If the health authority or trust are of the opinion that a particular voluntary organisation is likely to be able to give the parent advice or assistance in connection with any special educational needs that the child may have, they shall inform the parent accordingly.

Special educational needs tribunal

177.–(1) There shall be established a tribunal, to be known as the Special Educational Needs Tribunal (referred to in this Part of this Act as 'the Tribunal'), to exercise the jurisdiction conferred on it by this Part of this Act.

(2) There shall be appointed–

    (a) a President of the Tribunal (referred to in this Part of this Act as 'the President'),

    (b) a panel of persons (referred to in this Part of this Act as 'the chairmen's panel') who may serve as chairman of the Tribunal, and

    (c) a panel of persons (referred to in this Part of this Act as 'the lay panel') who may serve as the other two members of the Tribunal apart from the chairman.

(3) The President and the members of the chairmen's panel shall each be appointed by the Lord Chancellor.

(4) The members of the lay panel shall each be appointed by the Secretary of State.

(5) Regulations may–

    (a) provide for the jurisdiction of the Tribunal to be exercised by such number of tribunals as may be determined from time to time by the President, and

    (b) make such other provision in connection with the establishment and continuation of the Tribunal as the Secretary of State considers necessary or desirable.

(6) The Secretary of State may, with the consent of the Treasury, provide such staff and accommodation as the Tribunal may require.

Schedule 9
ATTENDANCE AT EXAMINATIONS

4.–(1) Where a local education authority propose to make an assessment, they may serve a notice on the parent of the child concerned requiring the child's attendance for examination in accordance with the provisions of the notice.

(2) The parent of a child examined under this paragraph may be present at the examination if he so desires.

(3) A notice under this paragraph shall–

(a) state the purpose of the examination,

(b) state the time and place at which the examination will be held,

(c) name an officer of the authority from whom further information may be obtained,

(d) inform the parent that he may submit such information to the authority as he may wish, and

(e) inform the parent of his right to be present at the examination.

OFFENCE

5.–(1) Any parent who fails without reasonable excuse to comply with any requirements of a notice served on him under paragraph 4 above commits an offence if the notice relates to a child who is not over compulsory school age at the time stated in it as the time for holding the examination.

(2) A person guilty of an offence under this paragraph is liable on summary conviction to a fine not exceeding level 2 on the standard scale.

Schedule 10: Making and maintenance of statements under section 168
INTRODUCTORY

1. In this Schedule, 'statement' means a statement of a child's special educational needs under section 168 of this Act.

COPY OF PROPOSED STATEMENT

2. Before making a statement, a local education authority shall serve on the parent of the child concerned–

(a) a copy of the proposed statement, and

(b) a written notice explaining the arrangements under paragraph 3 below, the effect of paragraph 4 below and the right to appeal under section 170 of this Act and containing such other information as may be prescribed,

but the copy of the proposed statement shall not specify any matter in pursuance of section 168(4) of this Act or any prescribed matter.

CHOICE OF SCHOOL

3.–(1) Every local education authority shall make arrangements for enabling a parent on whom a copy of a proposed statement has been served under paragraph 2 above to express a preference as to the maintained, grant-maintained or grant-maintained special school at which he wishes education to be provided for his child and to give reasons for his preference.

(2) Any such preference must be expressed or made within the period of fifteen days beginning–

> (a) with the date on which the written notice mentioned in paragraph 2(b) above was served on the parent, or

> (b) if a meeting has (or meetings have) been arranged under paragraph 4(1)(b) or (2) below, with the date fixed for that meeting (or the last of those meetings).

(3) Where a local education authority make a statement in a case where the parent of the child concerned has expressed a preference in pursuance of such arrangements as to the school at which he wishes education to be provided for his child, they shall specify the name of that school in the statement unless–

> (a) the school is unsuitable to the child's age, ability or aptitude or to his special educational needs, or

> (b) the attendance of the child at the school would be incompatible with the provision of efficient education for the children with whom he would be educated or the efficient use of resources.

(4) A local education authority shall, before specifying the name of any maintained, grant-maintained or grant-maintained special school in a statement, consult the governing body of the school and, if the school is maintained by another local education authority, that authority.

REPRESENTATIONS

4.–(1) A parent on whom a copy of a proposed statement has been served under paragraph 2 above may–

> (a) make representations (or further representations) to the local education authority about the content of the statement, and

> (b) require the authority to arrange a meeting between him and an officer of the authority at which the statement can be discussed.

(2) Where a parent, having attended a meeting arranged by a local education authority under sub-paragraph (1)(b) above, disagrees with any part of the assessment in question, he may require the authority to arrange such meeting or meetings as they consider will enable him to discuss the relevant advice with the appropriate person or persons.

(3) In this paragraph–

> 'relevant advice' means such of the advice given to the authority in connection with the assessment as they consider to be relevant to that part of the assessment with which the parent disagrees, and

> 'appropriate person' means the person who gave the relevant advice or any other person who, in the opinion of the authority, is the appropriate person to discuss it with the parent.

(4) Any representations under sub-paragraph (1)(a) above must be made within the period of fifteen days beginning–

> (a) with the date on which the written notice mentioned in paragraph 2(b) above was served on the parent, or

(b) if a meeting has (or meetings have) been arranged under sub-paragraph (1)(b) or (2) above, with the date fixed for that meeting (or the last of those meetings).

(5) A requirement under sub-paragraph (1)(b) above must be made within the period of fifteen days beginning with the date on which the written notice mentioned in paragraph 2(b) above was served on the parent.

(6) A requirement under sub-paragraph (2) above must be made within the period of fifteen days beginning with the date fixed for the meeting arranged under sub-paragraph (1)(b) above.

MAKING THE STATEMENT

5.–(1) Where representations are made to a local education authority under paragraph 4(1)(a) above, the authority shall not make the statement until they have considered the representations and the period or the last of the periods allowed by paragraph 4 above for making requirements or further representations has expired.

(2) The statement may be in the form originally proposed (except as to the matters required to be excluded from the copy of the proposed statement) or in a form modified in the light of the representations.

(3) Regulations may provide that, where a local education authority are under a duty (subject to compliance with the preceding requirements of this Schedule) to make a statement, the duty, or any step required to be taken for performance of the duty, must, subject to prescribed exceptions, be performed within the prescribed period.

(4) Such provision shall not relieve the authority of the duty to make a statement, or take any step, which has not been performed or taken within that period.

SERVICE OF STATEMENT

6. Where a local education authority make a statement they shall serve a copy of the statement on the parent of the child concerned and shall give notice in writing to him–

(a) of his right under section 170(1) of this Act to appeal against the description in the statement of the authority's assessment of the child's special educational needs, the special educational provision specified in the statement or, if no school is named in the statement, that fact, and

(b) of the name of the person to whom he may apply for information and advice about the child's special educational needs.

KEEPING, DISCLOSURE AND TRANSFER OF STATEMENTS

7.–(1) Regulations may make provision as to the keeping and disclosure of statements.

(2) Regulations may make provision, where a local education authority become responsible for a child for whom a statement is maintained by another authority, for the transfer of the statement to them and for Part III of this Act to have effect as if the duty to maintain the transferred statement were their duty.

CHANGE OF NAMED SCHOOL

8.–(1) Sub-paragraph (2) below applies where–

(a) the parent of a child for whom a statement is maintained which specifies the name of a school or institution asks the local education authority to substitute for that name the name of a maintained, grant-maintained or grant-maintained special school specified by the parent, and

(b) the request is not made less than twelve months after–

    (i) a request under this paragraph,

    (ii) the service of a copy of the statement under paragraph 6 above,

    (iii) if the statement has been amended, the date when notice of the amendment is given under paragraph 10(3)(b) below, or

    (iv) if the parent has appealed to the Tribunal under section 170 of this Act or this paragraph, the date when the appeal is concluded,

whichever is the later.

(2) The local education authority shall comply with the request unless–

(a) the school is unsuitable to the child's age, ability or aptitude or to his special educational needs, or

(b) the attendance of the child at the school would be incompatible with the provision of efficient education for the children with whom he would be educated or the efficient use of resources.

(3) Where the local education authority determine not to comply with the request–

(a) they shall give notice of that fact and of the effect of paragraph (b) below to the parent of the child, and

(b) the parent of the child may appeal to the Tribunal against the determination.

(4) On the appeal the Tribunal may–

(a) dismiss the appeal, or

(b) order the local education authority to substitute for the name of the school or other institution specified in the statement the name of the school specified by the parent.

(5) Regulations may provide that, where a local education authority are under a duty to comply with a request under this paragraph, the duty must, subject to prescribed exceptions, be performed within the prescribed period.

(6) Such provision shall not relieve the authority of the duty to comply with such a request which has not been complied with within that period.

PROCEDURE FOR AMENDING OR CEASING TO MAINTAIN A STATEMENT

9.–(1) A local education authority may not amend, or cease to maintain, a statement except in accordance with paragraph 10 or 11 below.

(2) Sub-paragraph (1) above does not apply where the local education authority–

(a) cease to maintain a statement for a child who has ceased to be a child for whom they are responsible,

(b) amend a statement in pursuance of paragraph 8 above,

(c) are ordered to cease to maintain a statement under section 170(3)(c) of this Act, or

(d) amend a statement in pursuance of directions under section 197 of this Act.

10.–(1) Before amending a statement, a local education authority shall serve on the parent of the child concerned a notice informing him–

(a) of their proposal, and

(b) of his right to make representations under sub-paragraph (2) below.

(2) A parent on whom a notice has been served under sub-paragraph (1) above may, within the period of fifteen days beginning with the date on which the notice is served, make representations to the local education authority about their proposal.

(3) The local education authority–

(a) shall consider any representations made to them under sub-paragraph (2) above, and

(b) on taking a decision on the proposal to which the representations relate, shall give notice in writing to the parent of their decision.

(4) Where a local education authority make an amendment under this paragraph to the description in a statement of the authority's assessment of a child's special educational needs or to the special educational provision specified in a statement, they shall give notice in writing to the parent of his right under section 170(1) of this Act to appeal against the description in the statement of the authority's assessment of the child's special educational needs, the special educational provision specified in the statement or, if no school is named in the statement, that fact.

(5) A local education authority may only amend a statement under this paragraph within the prescribed period beginning with the service of the notice under sub-paragraph (1) above.

11.–(1) A local education authority may cease to maintain a statement only if it is no longer necessary to maintain it.

(2) where the local education authority determine to cease to maintain a statement–

(a) they shall give notice of that fact and of the effect of paragraph (b) below to the parent of the child, and

(b) the parent of the child may appeal to the Tribunal against the determination.

(3) On an appeal under this paragraph the Tribunal may–

(a) dismiss the appeal, or

(b) order the local education authority to continue to maintain the statement in its existing form or with such amendments of the description in the statement of the authority's assessment of the child's special educational needs or the special educational provision specified in the statement, and such other consequential amendments, as the Tribunal may determine.

(4) Except where the parent of the child appeals to the Tribunal under this paragraph, a local education authority may only cease to maintain a statement under this paragraph within the prescribed period beginning with the service of the notice under sub-paragraph (2) above.

PART I: GENERAL ASSESSMENT REGULATIONS (1994 1047)

Title and commencement

1. These Regulations may be cited as the Education (Special Educational Needs) Regulations 1994 and shall come into force on 1st September 1994.

Interpretation

2. –(1) In these Regulations –

'the Act' means the Education Act 1993;

'authority' means a local education authority;

'district health authority' has the same meaning as in the National Health Service Act 1977**(c)**;

'head teacher' includes any person to whom the duties or functions of a head teacher under these Regulations have been delegated by the head teacher in accordance with regulation 3;

'social services authority' means a local authority for the purposes of the Local Authority Social Services Act 1970**(d)** acting in the discharge of such functions as are referred to in section 2(1) of that Act;

'target' means the knowledge, skills and understanding which a child is expected to have by the end of a particular period;

'transition plan' means a document prepared pursuant to regulation 16(9) or 17(9) which sets out the arrangements which an authority consider appropriate for a young person during the period when he is aged 14 to 19 years, including arrangements for special educational provision and for any other necessary provision, for suitable employment and accommodation and for leisure activities, and which will facilitate a satisfactory transition from childhood to adulthood;

(c) 1977 c.49; section 8 was amended by paragraph 28 of Schedule 1 to the Health Services Act 1980 (c.53) and by sections 1(1) of and Schedule 10 to the National Health Service and Community Care Act 1990 (c.19); the definition of 'district health authority' in section 128(1) was substituted by section 26(1) and (2)(b) of the National Health Service and Community Care Act 1990.

(d) 1970 c.42; section 1 was amended by section 195(1) of the Local Government Act 1972 (c.70).

'working day' means a day other than a Saturday, Sunday, Christmas Day, Good Friday or Bank Holiday within the meaning of the Banking and Financial Dealings Act 1971(e);

'the 1981 Act' means the Education Act 1981(f);

'the 1983 Regulations' means the Education (Special Educational Needs) Regulations 1983(g).

(2) In these Regulations any reference to the district health authority or the social services authority is, in relation to a particular child, a reference to the district health authority or social services authority in whose area that child lives.

(3) Where a thing is required to be done under these Regulations –

(a) within a period after an action is taken, the day on which that action was taken shall not be counted in the calculation of that period; and

(b) within a period and the last day of that period is not a working day, the period shall be extended to include the following working day.

(4) References in these Regulations to a section are references to a section of the Act.

(5) References in these Regulations to a regulation are references to a regulation in these Regulations and references to a Schedule are references to the Schedule to these Regulations.

Delegation of functions

3. Where a head teacher has any functions or duties under these Regulations he may delegate those functions or duties –

(a) generally to a member of the staff of the school who is a qualified teacher, or

(b) in a particular case to a member of the staff of the school who teaches the child in question.

Service of documents

4. –(1) Where any provision in Part III of the Act or in these Regulations authorises or requires any document to be served on or sent to a person or any written notice to be given to a person the document may be served or sent or the notice may be given by properly addressing, pre-paying and posting a letter containing the document or notice.

(2) For the purposes of this regulation, the proper address of a person is –

(a) in the case of the child's parent, his last known address;

(b) in the case of a head teacher or other member of the staff of a school, the school's address;

(c) in the case of any other person, the last known address of the place where he carries on his business, profession or other employment.

(e) 1971 c.80.

(f) 1981 c.60.

(g) S.1. 1983/29, amended by S.1. 1988/1067 and 1990/1524.

(3) Where first class post is used, the document or notice shall be treated as served, sent or given on the second working day after the date of posting, unless the contrary is shown.

(4) Where second class post is used, the document or notice shall be treated as served, sent or given on the fourth working day after the date of posting, unless the contrary is shown.

(5) The date of posting shall be presumed, unless the contrary is shown, to be the date shown in the post-mark on the envelope in which the document is contained.

PART II: ASSESSMENTS

Notices relating to assessment

5. –(1) Where under section 167(1) or 174(2) an authority give notice to a child's parent that they propose to make an assessment, or under section 167(4) give notice to a child's parent of their decision to make an assessment, they shall send copies of the relevant notice to –

(a) the social services authority,

(b) the district health authority, and

(c) if the child is registered at a school, the head teacher of that school.

(2) Where a copy of a notice is sent under paragraph (1) an endorsement on the copy or a notice accompanying that copy shall inform the recipient what help the authority are likely to request.

(3) Where under section 172(2) or 173(1) a child's parent asks the authority to arrange for an assessment to be made the authority shall give notice in writing to the person referred to in paragraph (1)(a) to (c) of the fact that the request has been made and inform them what help they are likely to request.

Advice to be sought

6. –(1) For the purpose of making an assessment under section 167 an authority shall seek –

(a) advice from the child's parent;

(b) educational advice as provided for in regulation 7;

(c) medical advice from the district health authority as provided for in regulation 8;

(d) psychological advice as provided for in regulation 9;

(e) advice from the social services authority; and

(f) any other advice which the authority consider appropriate for the purpose of arriving at a satisfactory assessment.

(2) The advice referred to in paragraph (1) shall be written advice relating to –

(a) the educational, medical, psychological or other features of the case (according to the nature of the advice sought) which appear to be relevant to the child's educational needs (including his likely future needs);

(b) how those features could affect the child's educational needs, and

(c) the provision which is appropriate for the child in light of those features of the child's case, whether by way of special educational provision or non-educational provision, but not relating to any matter which is required to be specified in a statement by virtue of section 168(4)(b).

(3) A person from whom the advice referred to in paragraph (1) is sought may in connection therewith consult such persons as it appears to him expedient to consult; and he shall consult such persons, if any, as are specified in the particular case by the authority as persons who have relevant knowledge of, or information relating to, the child.

(4) When seeking the advice referred to in paragraph (1)(b) to (f) an authority shall provide the person from whom it is sought with copies of –

(a) any representations made by the parent, and

(b) any evidence submitted by, or at the request of, the parent under section 167(1)(d).

(5) The authority need not seek the advice referred to in paragraph (1)(b), (c), (d), (e) or (f) if –

(a) the authority have obtained advice under paragraph (1)(b), (c), (d), (e) or (f) respectively within the preceding 12 months, and

(b) the authority, the person from whom the advice was obtained and the child's parent are satisfied that the existing advice is sufficient for the purpose of arriving at a satisfactory assessment.

Educational advice

7. –(1) The educational advice referred to in regulation 6(1)(b) shall, subject to paragraphs (2) to (5), be sought –

(a) from the head teacher of each school which the child is currently attending or which he has attended at any time within the preceding 18 months;

(b) if advice cannot be obtained from a head teacher of a school which the child is currently attending (because the child is not attending a school or otherwise) from a person who the authority are satisfied has experience of teaching children with special educational needs or knowledge of the differing provision which may be called for in different cases to meet those needs;

(c) if the child is not currently attending a school and if advice obtained under subparagraph (b) is not advice from such a person, from a person responsible for educational provision for him; and

(d) if any of the child's parents is a serving member of Her Majesty's armed forces, from the Service Children's Education Authority.

(2) The advice sought as provided in paragraph (1) shall not be sought from any person who is not a qualified teacher within the meaning of section 218 of the Education Reform Act 1988**(h)**.

(3) The advice sought from a head teacher as provided in paragraph (1)(a) shall, if the head teacher has not himself taught the child within the preceding 18 months, be advice given after consultation with a teacher who has so taught the child.

(4) The advice sought from a head teacher as provided in paragraph (1)(a) shall include advice relating to the steps which have been taken by the school to identify and assess the special educational needs of the child and to make provision for the purpose of meeting those needs.

(5) here it appears to the authority, in consequence of medical advice or otherwise, that the child in question is –

(a) hearing impaired, or

(b) visually impaired, or

(c) both hearing impaired and visually impaired,

and any person from whom advice is sought as provided in paragraph (1) is not qualified to teach pupils who are so impaired then the advice sought shall be advice given after consultation with a person who is so qualified.

(6) For the purposes of paragraph (5) a person shall be considered to be qualified to teach pupils who are hearing impaired or visually impaired or who are both hearing impaired and visually impaired if he is qualified to be employed at a school as a teacher of a class for pupils who are so impaired otherwise than to give instruction in a craft, trade, or domestic subject.

(7) Paragraphs (3) and (5) are without prejudice to regulation 6(3).

Medical advice

8. The advice referred to in paragraph 6(1)(c) shall be sought from the district health authority, who shall obtain the advice from a fully registered medical practitioner.

Psychological advice

9. –(1) The psychological advice referred to in regulation 6(1)(d) shall be sought from a person –

(a) regularly employed by the authority as an educational psychologist, or

(b) engaged by the authority as an educational psychologist in the case in question.

(2) The advice sought from a person as provided in paragraph (1) shall, if that person has reason to believe that another psychologist has relevant knowledge of, or information relating to, the child, be advice given after consultation with that other psychologist.

(3) Paragraph (2) is without prejudice to regulation 6(3).

Matters to be taken into account in making an assessment

10. When making an assessment an authority shall take into consideration –

(a) any representations made by the child's parent under section 167(1)(d);

(h) 1988 c.40.

(b) any evidence submitted by, or at the request of, the child's parent under section 167(1)(d); and

(c) the advice obtained under regulation 6.

Time limits

11. –(1) Where under section 167(1) the authority serve a notice on the child's parent informing him that they propose to make an assessment of the child's educational needs under section 167 they shall within 6 weeks of the date of service of the notice give notice to the child's parent –

(a) under section 167(4) of their decision to make an assessment, and of their reasons for making that decision, or

(b) under section 167(6) of their decision not to assess the educational needs of the child.

(2) Where under section 174(2) the authority serve a notice on the child's parent informing him that they propose to make an assessment of the child's educational needs under section 167 they shall within 6 weeks of the date of service of the notice give notice to the child's parent and to the governing body of the grant-maintained school which asked the authority to make an assessment –

(a) under section 174(5) of their decision to make an assessment and their reasons for making that decision, or

(b) under section 174(6) of their decision not to assess the educational needs of the child.

(3) Where under sections 172(2) or 173(1) a parent asks the authority to arrange for an assessment to be made under section 167 they shall within 6 weeks of the date of receipt of the request give notice to the child's parent –

(a) under section 167(4) of their decision to make an assessment, or

(b) under section 172(3)(a) or 173(2)(a) respectively of their decision not to comply with the request and of the parent's right to appeal to the Tribunal against the determination.

(4) An authority need not comply with the time limits referred to in paragraphs (1) to (3) if it is impractical to do so because –

(a) the authority have requested advice from the head teacher of a school during a period beginning one week before any date on which that school was closed for a continuous period of not less than 4 weeks from that date and ending one week before the date on which it re-opens;

(b) exceptional personal circumstances affect the child or his parent during the 6 week period referred to in paragraphs (1) to (3); or

(c) the child or his parent are absent from the area of the authority for a continuous period of not less than 4 weeks during the 6 week period referred to in paragraphs (1) to (3).

(5) Subject to paragraph (6), where under section 167(4) an authority have given notice to the child's parent of their decision to make an assessment they

shall complete that assessment within 10 weeks of the date on which such notice was given.

(6) An authority need not comply with the time limit referred to in paragraph (5) if it is impractical to do so because –

(a) in exceptional cases after receiving advice sought under regulation 6 it is necessary for the authority to seek further advice;

(b) the child's parent has indicated to the authority that he wishes to provide advice to the authority after the expiry of 6 weeks from the date on which a request for such advice under regulation 6(a) was received, and the authority have agreed to consider such advice before completing the assessment;

(c) the authority have requested advice from the head teacher of a school under regulation 6(1)(b) during a period beginning one week before any date on which that school was closed for a continuous period of not less than 4 weeks from that date and ending one week before the date on which it re-opens;

(d) the authority have requested advice from a district health authority or a social services authority under regulation 6(1)(c) or (e) respectively and the district health authority or the social services authority have not complied with that request within 6 weeks from the date on which it was made;

(e) exceptional personal circumstances affect the child or his parent during the 10 week period referred to in paragraph (5);

(f) the child or his parent are absent from the area of the authority for a continuous period of not less than 4 weeks during the 10 week period referred to in paragraph (5); or

(g) the child fails to keep an appointment for an examination or a test during the 10 week period referred to in paragraph (5).

(7) Subject to paragraph (8), where an authority have requested advice from a district health authority or a social services authority under regulation 6(1)(c) or (e) respectively they shall comply with that request within 6 weeks of the date on which they receive it.

(8) A district health authority or a social services authority need not comply with the time limit referred to in paragraph (7) if it is impractical to do so because –

(a) exceptional personal circumstances affect the child or his parent during the 6 week period referred to in paragraph (7);

(b) the child or his parent are absent from the area of the authority for a continuous period of not less than 4 weeks during the 6 week period referred to in paragraph (7);

(c) the child fails to keep an appointment for an examination or a test made by the district health authority or the social services authority respectively during the 6 week period referred to in paragraph (7); or

(d) they have not before the date on which a copy of a notice has been served on them in accordance with regulation 5(1) or a notice has been served on them in accordance with regulation 5(3) produced or maintained any information or records relevant to the assessment of the child under section 167.

PART III: STATEMENTS

Notice accompanying a proposed statement

12. The notice which shall accompany a copy of a proposed statement served on the parent pursuant to paragraph 2 of Schedule 10 to the Act shall be in a form substantially corresponding to that set out in Part A of the Schedule and shall contain the information therein specified.

Statement of special educational needs

13. A statement of a child's special educational needs made under section 168(1) shall be in a form substantially corresponding to that set out in Part B of the Schedule, shall contain the information therein specified, and shall be dated and authenticated by the signature of a duly authorised officer of the authority concerned.

Time limits

14. –(1) Where under section 167 an authority have made an assessment of the educational needs of a child for whom no statement is maintained they shall within two weeks of the date on which the assessment was completed either –

(a) serve a copy of a proposed statement and a written notice on the child's parent under paragraph 2 of Schedule 10 to the Act, or

(b) give notice in writing to the child's parent under section 169(1) that they have decided not to make a statement and that he may appeal against that decision to the Tribunal.

(2) Where under section 167 an authority have made an assessment of the educational needs of a child for whom a statement is maintained they shall within two weeks of the date on which the assessment was completed –

(a) under paragraph 10(1) of Schedule 10 to the Act serve on the child's parent a notice that they propose to amend the statement and of his right to make representations;

(b) under paragraph 11(2) of Schedule 10 to the Act give notice to the child's parent that they have determined to cease to maintain the statement and of his right of appeal to the Tribunal; or

(c) serve on the child's parent a notice which informs him that they have determined not to amend the statement and their reasons for that determination, which is accompanied by copies of the professional advice obtained during the assessment, and which informs the child's parent that under section 170(1)(c) he may appeal to the Tribunal against the description in the statement of the authority's assessment of the child's special educational needs, the special educational provision specified in the statement or, if no school is named in the statement, that fact.

(3) Subject to paragraph (4), where an authority have served a copy of a proposed statement on the child's parent under paragraph 2 of Schedule 10 to the Act they shall within 8 weeks of the date on which the proposed statement was served serve a copy of the completed statement and a written notice on the child's parent under paragraph 6 of that Schedule, or give notice to the child's parent that they have decided not to make a statement.

(4) The authority need not comply with the time limit referred to in paragraph (3) if it is impractical to do so because –

(a) exceptional person circumstances affect the child or his parent during the 8 week period referred to in paragraph (3);

(b) the child or his parent are absent from the area of the authority for a continuous period of not less than 4 weeks during the 8 week period referred to in paragraph (3);

(c) the child's parent indicates that he wishes to make representations to the authority about the content of the statement under paragraph 4(1)(a) of Schedule 10 the to Act after the expiry of the 15 day period for making such representations provided for in paragraph 4(4) of that Schedule;

(d) a meeting between the child's parent and an officer of the authority has been held pursuant to paragraph 4(1)(b) of Schedule 10 to the Act and the child's parent has required that another such meeting be arranged or under paragraph 4(2) of that Schedule has required a meeting with the appropriate person under to be arranged; or

(e) the authority have sent a written request to the Secretary of State seeking his consent under section 189(5)(b) to the child being educated at an independent school which is not approved by him and such consent has not been received by the authority within two weeks of the date on which the request was sent.

(5) Where under paragraph 8(1) of Schedule 10 the Act the child's parent asks the authority to substitute for the name of a school or institution specified in a statement the name of another school specified by him and where the condition referred to in paragraph 8(1)(b) of that Schedule has been satisfied the authority shall within 8 weeks of the date on which the request was received either –

(a) comply with the request; or

(b) give notice to the child's parent under paragraph 8(3) of that Schedule that they have determined not to comply with the request and that he may appeal against that determination to the Tribunal.

(6) Where under paragraph 10(1) of Schedule 10 to the Act an authority serve a notice on the child's parent informing him of their proposal to amend a statement they shall not amend the statement after the expiry of 8 weeks from the date on which the notice was served.

(7) Where under paragraph 11(2) of Schedule 10 to the Act an authority give notice to the child's parent that they have determined to cease to maintain a statement they shall not cease to maintain the statement –

(a) before the expiry of the prescribed period during which the parent may appeal to the Tribunal against the determination, or

(b) after the expiry of 4 weeks from the end of that period.

Review of statement where child not aged 14 attends school

15. –(1) This regulation applies where –

(a) an authority review a statement under section 172(5) other than on the making of an assessment,

(b) the child concerned attends a school, and

(c) regulation 16 does not apply.

(2) The authority shall by notice in writing require the head teacher of the child's school to submit a report to them under this regulation by a specified date not less than two months from the date the notice is given and shall send a copy of the notice to the child's parent.

(3) The head teacher shall for the purpose of preparing the report referred to in paragraph (2) seek advice as to the matters referred to in paragraph (4) from –

(a) the child's parent;

(b) any person whose advice the authority consider appropriate for the purpose of arriving at a satisfactory report and whom they specify in the notice referred to in paragraph (2), and

(c) any person whose advice the head teacher considers appropriate for the purpose of arriving at a satisfactory report.

(4) The advice referred to in paragraph (3) shall be written advice as to –

(a) the child's progress towards meeting the objectives specified in the statement;

(b) the child's progress towards attaining any targets established in furtherance of the objectives specified in the statement;

(c) where the school is not established in a hospital and is a maintained, grant-maintained or grant-maintained special school, the application of the provisions of the National Curriculum to the child;

(d) where the school is not established in a hospital and is a maintained, grant-maintained or grant-maintained special school, the application of any provisions substituted for the provisions of the National Curriculum in order to maintain a balanced and broadly based curriculum;

(e) where appropriate, and in any case where a transition plan exists, any matters which are the appropriate subject of such a plan;

(f) whether the statement continues to be appropriate;

(g) any amendments to the statement which would be appropriate; and

(h) whether the authority should cease to maintain the statement.

(5) The notice referred to in paragraph (2) shall require the head teacher to invite the following persons to attend a meeting to be held on a date before the report referred to in that paragraph is submitted –

(a) the representative of the authority specified in the notice,

(b) the child's parent,

(c) a member or members of the staff of the school who teach the child or who are otherwise responsible for the provision of education for the child whose attendance the head teacher considers appropriate,

(d) any other person whose attendance the head teacher considers appropriate, and

(e) any person whose attendance the authority consider appropriate and who is specified in the notice.

(6) The head teacher shall not later than two weeks before the date on which a meeting referred to in paragraph (5) is to be held send to all the persons invited to that meeting copies of the advice he has received pursuant to his request under paragraph (3) and by written notice accompanying the copies shall request the recipients to submit to him before or at the meeting written comments on that advice and any other advice which they think appropriate.

(7) The meeting referred to in paragraph (5) shall consider –

(a) the matters referred to in paragraph (4); and

(b) any significant changes in the child's circumstances since the date on which the statement was made or last reviewed.

(8) The meeting shall recommend –

(a) any steps which it concludes ought to be taken, including whether the authority should amend or cease to maintain the statement,

(b) any targets to be established in furtherance of the objectives specified in the statement which it concludes the child ought to meet during the period until the next review, and

(c) where a transition plan exists, the matters which it concludes ought to be included in that plan.

(9) If the meeting cannot agree the recommendations to be made under paragraph (8) the persons who attended the meeting shall make differing recommendations as appears necessary to each of them.

(10) The report to be submitted under paragraph (2) shall be completed after the meeting is held and shall include the head teacher's assessment of the matters referred to in paragraph (7) and his recommendations as to the matters referred to in paragraph (8), and shall refer to any difference between his assessment and recommendations and those of the meeting.

(11) When the head teacher submits his report to the authority under paragraph (2) he shall at the same time send copies to –

(a) the child's parent,

(b) the persons from whom the head teacher sought advice under paragraph (3),

(c) the persons who were invited to attend the meeting in accordance with paragraph (5),

(d) any other person to whom the authority consider it appropriate that a copy be sent and to whom they direct him to send a copy, and

(e) any other person to whom the head teacher considers it appropriate that a copy be sent.

(12) The authority shall review the statement under section 172(5) in light of the report and any other information or advice which they consider relevant, shall make written recommendations as to the matters referred to in paragraph (8)(a) and (b) and, where a transition plan exists, shall amend the plan as they consider appropriate.

(13) The authority shall within one week of completing the review under section 172(5) end copies of the recommendations and any transition plan referred to in paragraph (12) to –

(a) the child's parent;

(b) the head teacher;

(c) the persons from whom the head teacher sought advice under paragraph (3);

(d) the persons who were invited to attend the meeting in accordance with paragraph (5), and

(e) any other person to whom the authority consider it appropriate that a copy be sent.

Review of statement where child aged 14 attends school

16. –(1) This regulation applies where –

(a) an authority review a statement under section 172(5) other than on the making of an assessment,

(b) the child concerned attends a school, and

(c) the review is the first review commenced after the child has attained the age of 14 years.

(2) The authority shall for the purpose of preparing a report under this regulation by notice in writing require the head teacher of the child's school to seek the advice referred to in regulation 15(4), including in all cases advice as to the matters referred to in regulation 15(4)(e), from –

(a) the child's parent,

(b) any person whose advice the authority consider appropriate for the purpose of arriving at a satisfactory report and whom they specify in the notice referred to above, and

(c) any person whose advice the head teacher considers appropriate for the purpose of arriving at a satisfactory report.

(3) The authority shall invite the following persons to attend a meeting to be held on a date before the review referred to in paragraph (1) is required to be completed –

(a) the child's parent;

(b) a member or members of the staff of the school who teach the child or who are otherwise responsible for the provision of education for the child whose attendance the head teacher considers appropriate and whom he has asked the authority to invite;

(c) a representative of the social services authority;

(d) a person providing careers services under sections 8 to 10 of the Employment and Training Act 1973**(i)**;

(e) any person whose attendance the head teacher considers appropriate and whom he has asked the authority to invite; and

(f) any person whose attendance the authority consider appropriate.

(4) The head teacher shall not later than two weeks before the date on which the meeting referred to in paragraph (3) is to be held serve on all the persons invited to attend that meeting copies of the advice he has received pursuant to his request under paragraph (2) and shall by written notice request the recipients to submit to him before or at the meeting written comments on that advice and any other advice which they think appropriate.

(5) A representative of the authority shall attend the meeting.

(6) the meeting shall consider the matters referred to in regulation 15(7), in all cases including the matters referred to in regulation 15(4)(e), and shall make recommendations in accordance with regulation 15(8) and (9), in all cases including recommendations as to the matters referred to in regulation 15(8)(c).

(7) The report to be prepared by the authority under paragraph (2) shall be completed after the meeting, shall contain the authority's assessment of the matters required to be considered by the meeting and their recommendations as to the matters required to be recommended by it and shall refer to any difference between their assessment and recommendations and those of the meeting.

(8) The authority shall within one week of the date on which the meeting was held send copies of the report completed under paragraph (7) to –

(a) the child's parent;

(b) the head teacher;

(c) the persons from whom the head teacher sought advice under paragraph (2);

(d) the persons who were invited to attend the meeting under paragraph (3); and

(e) any person to whom they consider it appropriate to send a copy.

(9) The authority shall review the statement under section 172(5) in light of the report and any other information or advice which it considers relevant, shall make written recommendations as to the matters referred to in regulation 15(8)(a) and (b), and shall prepare a transition plan.

(i) 1973 c.50. Sections 8 to 10 were replaced by section 45 of the Trade Union and Employment Rights Act 1993 (c.19).

(10) The authority shall within one week of completing the review under section 172(5) send copies of the recommendations and the transition plan referred to in paragraph (9) to the persons referred to in paragraph (8).

Review of statement where child does not attend school

17. –(1) This regulation applies where an authority review a statement under section 172(5) other than on the making of an assessment and the child concerned does not attend a school.

(2) The authority shall prepare a report addressing the matters referred to in regulation 15(4), including the matters referred to in regulation 15(4)(e) in any case where the review referred to in paragraph (1) is commenced after the child has attained the age of 14 years or older, and for that purpose shall seek advice on those matters from the child's parent and any other person whose advice they consider appropriate in the case in question for the purpose of arriving at a satisfactory report.

(3) The authority shall invite the following persons to attend a meeting to be held on a date before the review referred to in paragraph (1) is required to be completed –

(a) the child's parent;

(b) where the review referred to in paragraph (1) is the first review commenced after the child has attained the age of 14 years, a representative of the social services authority;

(c) where subparagraph (b) applies, a person providing careers services under sections 8 to 10 of the Employment and Training Act 1973; and

(d) any person or persons whose attendance the authority consider appropriate.

(4) The authority shall not later than two weeks before the date on which the meeting referred to in paragraph (3) is to be held send to all the persons invited to that meeting a copy of the report which they propose to make under paragraph (2) and by written notice accompanying the copies shall request the recipients to submit to the authority written comments on the report and any other advice which they think appropriate.

(5) A representative of the authority shall attend the meeting.

(6) The meeting shall consider the matters referred to in regulation 15(7), including in any case where the review is commenced after the child has attained the age of 14 years the matters referred to in regulation 15(4)(e), and shall make recommendations in accordance with regulation 15(8) and (9), including in any case where the child has attained the age of 14 years or older as aforesaid recommendations as to the matters referred to in regulation 15(8)(c).

(7) The report prepared by the authority under paragraph (2) shall be completed after the meeting referred to in paragraph (3) is held, shall contain the authority's assessment of the matters required to be considered by the meeting and their recommendations as to the matters required to be recommended by it, and shall refer to any difference between their assessment and recommendations and those of the meeting.

(8) The authority shall within one week of the date on which the meeting referred to in paragraph (3) was held send copies of the report completed under paragraph (7) to –

(a) the child's parent;

(b) the persons from whom they sought advice under paragraph (2);

(c) the persons who were invited to attend the meeting under paragraph (3); and

(d) any person to whom they consider it appropriate to send a copy.

(9) The authority shall review the statement under section 172(5) in light of the report and any other information or advice which it considers relevant, shall make written recommendations as to the matters referred to in regulation 15(8)(a) and (b), in any case where the review is the first review commenced after the child has attained the age of 14 years prepare a transition plan, and in any case where a transition plan exists amend the plan as they consider appropriate.

(10) The authority shall within one week of completing the review under section 172(5) send copies of the recommendations and any transition plan referred to in paragraph (9) to the persons referred to in paragraph (8).

Transfer of statements

18. –(1) This regulation applies where a child in respect of whom a statement is maintained moves from the area of the authority which maintains the statement ('the old authority') into that of another ('the new authority').

(2) The old authority shall transfer the statement to the new authority, and from the date of the transfer –

(a) the statement shall be treated for the purposes of the new authority's duties and functions under Part III of the Act and these Regulations as if it had been made by the new authority on the date on which it was made by the old authority, and

(b) where the new authority make an assessment under section 167 and the old authority have supplied the new authority with advice obtained in pursuance of a previous assessment regulation 6(5) shall apply as if the new authority had obtained the advice on the date on which the old authority obtained it.

(3) The new authority shall within 6 weeks of the date of the transfer serve a notice on the child's parent informing him –

(a) that the statement has been transferred,

(b) whether they propose to make an assessment under section 167, and

(c) when they propose to review the statement in accordance with paragraph (4).

(4) The new authority shall review the statement under section 172(5) before the expiry of whichever of the following two periods expires later –

(a) the period of twelve months beginning with the making of the statement, or as the case may be, with the previous review, or

(b) the period of three months beginning with the date of the transfer.

(5) Where by virtue of the transfer the new authority come under a duty to arrange the child's attendance at a school specified in the statement but in light of the child's move that attendance is no longer practicable the new authority may arrange for the child's attendance at another school appropriate for the child until such time as it is possible to amend the statement in accordance with paragraph 10 of Schedule 10 to the Act.

Restriction on disclosure of statements

19. –(1) Subject to the provision of the Act and of these Regulations, a statement in respect of a child shall not be disclosed without the parent's consent except –

(a) to persons to whom, in the opinion of the authority concerned, the statement should be disclosed in the interests of the child;

(b) for the purposes of any appeal under the Act;

(c) for the purposes of educational research which, in the opinion of the authority, may advance the education of children with special educational needs, if, but only if, the person engaged in that research undertakes not to publish anything contained in, or derived from, a statement otherwise than in a form which does not identify any individual concerned including, in particular, the child concerned and his parent;

(d) on the order of any court or for the purposes of any criminal proceedings;

(e) for the purposes of any investigation under Part III of the Local Government Act 1974 (investigation of maladministration)**(j)**;

(f) to the Secretary of State when he requests such disclosure for the purposes of deciding whether to give directions or make an order under section 68 or 99 of the Education Act 1944**(k)**;

(g) for the purposes of an assessment of the needs of the child with respect to the provision of any statutory services for him being carried out by officers of a social services authority by virtue of arrangements made

---

(j) 1974 c.7; Part III has been amended by paragraph 9(1) of Schedule 10 to the Community Land Act 1975 (c.77), by paragraph 14 of Schedule 22 and Part XI of Schedule 34 to the Local Government, Planning and Land Act 1980 (c.65), by paragraph 51(a) of Schedule 14 to the Local Government Act 1985 (c.51), by paragraph 4 of Schedule 3 to the Local Government Act 1988 (c.9), by paragraph 19 of Schedule 17 to the Housing Act 1988 (c.50), by sections 23(1), 25, 194(1) and (4), and 195(2) of, and paragraph 38 of Schedule 11 and Part II of Schedule 12 to, the Local Government and Housing Act 1989 (c.42), by section 1(6) of and paragraph 12 of Schedule 1 and paragraph 3 of Schedule 26 to the Water Act 1989 (c.15), and by section 2(1) of and paragraph 25 of Schedule 1 to the Water Consolidation (Consequential Provisions) Act 1991 (c.60).

(k) 1944 c.31.

under section 5(5) of the Disabled Persons (Services, Consultation and Representation) Act 1986**(l)**;

(h) for the purposes of a local authority in the performance of their duties under sections 22(3)(a), 85(4)(a), 86(3)(a) and 87(3) of the Children Act 1989**(m)**; or

(i) to one of Her Majesty's Inspectors of Schools, or to a registered inspector or a member of an inspection team, who requests the right to inspect or take copies of a statement in accordance with section 3(3) of or paragraph 7 of Schedule 2 to the Education (Schools) Act 1992**(n)** respectively.

(2) The arrangements for keeping such statements shall be such as to ensure, so far as is reasonably practicable, that unauthorised persons do not have access to them.

(3) In this regulation any reference to a statement includes a reference to any representations, evidence, advice or information which is set out in the appendices to a statement.

PART IV: REVOCATION AND TRANSITIONAL PROVISIONS

Revocation of the 1983 Regulations

20. Subject to regulation 21, the 1983 Regulations, the Education (Special Educational Needs) (Amendment) Regulations 1988 **(o)** and the Education (Special Educational Needs) (Amendment) Regulations 1990 **(p)** are hereby revoked.

Transitional provisions

21.-(1) Subject to the following provisions of this regulation references in these Regulations to anything done under the Act or these Regulations shall be read in relation to the times, circumstances or purposes in relation to which a corresponding provision of the 1981 Act of the 1983 Regulations had effect and so far as the nature of the reference permits as including a reference to that corresponding provision.

(2) Regulations 3 to 8 of the 1983 Regulations shall continue to apply in relation to any assessment where before 1st September 1994 in pursuance of section 5(5) of the 1981 Act the authority notify the parent that they have decided to make an assessment, and Part II of these Regulations shall not apply in relation to any such assessment.

(3) Where regulations 3 to 8 of the 1983 Regulations continue to apply in relation to any assessment but the authority have not before 1st January 1995 –

(l) 1986 c.33.

(m) 1989 c.41.

(n) 1992 c.38; paragraph 7 of Schedule 2 was amended by the Education Act 1993 (c.35), Schedule 19 paragraph 173(4).

(o) S.I. 1988/1067.

(p) S.I. 1990/1524.

(a) notified the parent of their decision that they are not required to determine the special educational provision of the child in accordance with section 5(7) of the 1981 Act, or

(b) served on the parent a copy of a proposed statement in accordance with section 7(3) of the 1981 Act

Part II of these Regulations shall apply in relation to the assessment from 1st January 1995 as if on that date the authority had given notice to the parent under section 167(4) of their decision to make an assessment.

(4) Where in accordance with paragraph (3) above Part II of these Regulations applies in relation to an assessment the authority shall obtain advice in accordance with Part II, but advice obtained in accordance with the 1983 Regulations shall be considered to have been obtained under Part II if such advice is appropriate for the purpose of arriving at a satisfactory assessment under that Part.

(5) Where before 1st September 1994 in accordance with section 5(3) of the 1981 Act the authority have served notice on the child's parent that they propose to make an assessment but they have not before that date notified the parent under section 5(5) of the 1981 Act that they have decided to make the assessment or notified them that they have decided not to make the assessment, the authority shall decide whether or not to make the assessment in accordance with section 167 and not later than 13th October 1994 give notice to the child's parent –

(a) under section 167(4) of their decision to make an assessment, and of their reasons for making that decision, or

(b) under section 167(6) of their decision not to assess the educational needs of the child

and Part II of these Regulations shall apply to any such assessment.

(6) Where before 1st September 1994 in accordance with section 9 of the 1981 Act a parent has asked the authority to arrange for an assessment to be made of the child's educational needs but the authority have not before that date notified the parent under section 5(5) of the 1981 Act that they have decided to make the assessment or notified them that they have decided not to make the assessment, the authority shall decide whether or not to make the assessment in accordance with section 167 and not later than 13th October 1994 give notice to the child's parent –

(a) under section 167(4) of their decision to make an assessment, or

(b) under section 172(30)(a) or 173(a) of their decision not to comply with the request and of the parent's right to appeal to the Tribunal against the determination.

and Part II of these Regulations shall apply to any such assessment.

(7) Regulation 10 of the 1983 Regulations shall continue to apply to the making of any statement where before 1st January 1995 the authority have served on the parent a copy of a proposed statement in accordance with section 7(3) of the 1981 Act, and regulations 12, 13 and 14(1) to (4) of these Regulations shall not apply to the making of any such statement.

(8) Regulation 14(6) and (7) shall not apply in relation to a proposal to amend or cease to maintain a statement where an authority serve a notice under paragraph 6 of Schedule 1 to the 1981 Act(q) before 1st September 1994.

(9) Regulations 15 to 17 shall not apply to any review of a statement which is required to be completed before 1st December 1994.

(10) Regulations 15 to 17 shall apply to a review of a statement which is not required to be completed before 1st December 1994, but where the statement was made under the 1981 Act they shall apply with any necessary modifications, including the following:

    (a)where the review is the first review commenced after 1st September 1994 –

        (i)the authority shall seek advice as to the objectives which the special educational provision for the child should meet rather than as to the child's progress towards meeting the objectives specified in the statement;

        (ii)the authority shall seek advice as to the targets which should be established in furtherance of those objectives rather than as to the child's progress towards attaining any such targets;

        (iii)where the child has attained the age of 14 years before the date on which the review is commenced the authority shall in any event seek advice as to any matters which are the appropriate subject of a transition plan;

        (iv)the meeting held in accordance with regulations 15(7), 16(6) or 17(6) shall consider the matters referred to in those regulations as modified by subparagraphs (i) to (iii) above as appropriate, and shall make recommendations under regulation 15(8), 16(7) or 17(7) but including recommendations as to the objectives referred to in subparagraph (i), the targets referred to in subparagraph (ii) and where appropriate the transition plan referred to in paragraph (iii); and

        (v)the authority shall review the statement in accordance with regulation 15(12), 16(9) or 17(9), shall make recommendations as to the matters referred to in those regulations read in light of the modifications in this subparagraph, shall prepare a transition plan where subparagraph (iii) above applies, and shall in any event specify the objectives referred to in subparagraph (i) above;

and

    (b)where the review is not the first review commenced after 1st September 1994 any reference to objectives shall include a reference to objectives

---

(q) Paragraph 6(4) of Schedule 1 was added by the Education Reform Act 1988 (c.40), Schedule 12, paragraph 85.

specified in accordance with subparagraph (a)(v) above in addition to objectives specified in a statement.

(11) Subject to paragraphs (12) and (13), regulation 12 of the 1983 Regulations shall continue to apply in relation to a transfer on a date before 1st September 1994, and regulation 18 of these Regulations shall not apply in relation to such a transfer.

(12) Notwithstanding paragraph (11), where a statement has been transferred on a date before 1st September 1994 and the new authority has not before that date either –

(a) in pursuance of section 5(3) of the 1981 Act served a notice on the child's parent that they propose to make an assessment, or

(b) in pursuance of regulation 12(4) of the 1983 Regulations notified the child's parent that they do not propose to make an assessment,

they shall comply with regulation 18(3) of these Regulations before 13th October 1994.

(13) Notwithstanding paragraph (11), where a statement has been transferred on a date before 1st September 1994 the new authority shall review the statement under section 172(5) before the expiry of whichever of the following tow periods expires later –

(a) the period of twelve months beginning with the making of the statement, or as the case may be, with the previous review, or

(b) the period ending on 30th November 1994.

(14) Regulation 11 of the 1983 Regulations shall not apply to statements made before or after 1st September 1994 and regulation 19 of these Regulations shall apply, except that a statement may be disclosed for the purposes of any appeal under section 8 of the 1981 Act(r) as well as for the purposes of any appeal under the Act.

SCHEDULE: PART A: NOTICE TO PARENT

To: [*name and address of parent*]

1. Accompanying this notice is a copy of a statement of the special educational needs of [*name of child*] which [*name of authority*] ('the authority') propose to make under the Education Act 1993.

2. You may express a preference for the maintained, grant-maintained or grant-maintained special school you wish your child to attend and may give reasons for your preference.

3. If you wish to express such a preference you must do so not later than 15 days from the date on which you receive this notice and the copy of the statement or 15 days from the date on which you last attend a meeting in accordance with paragraph 10 or 11 below, whichever is later. If the 15th day

---

(r) Section 8(1) was substituted by the Education Reform Act 1988 (c.40), Schedule 12, paragraph 84.

falls on a weekend or a bank holiday you must do so not later than the following working day.

4. If you express a preference in accordance with paragraphs 2 and 3 above the authority are required to specify the name of the school you prefer in the statement, and accordingly to arrange special educational provision at that school, unless –

(a) the school is unsuitable to your child's age, ability or aptitude or to his/her special educational needs, or

(b) the attendance of your child at the school would be incompatible with the provision of efficient education for the children with whom he/she would be educated or the efficient use of resources.

5. The authority will normally arrange special educational provision in a maintained, grant-maintained or grant-maintained special school. However, if you believe that the authority should arrange special educational provision for your child at a non-maintained special school or an independent school you may make representations to that effect.

6. The following maintained, grant-maintained and grant-maintained special schools provide [*primary/secondary*] education in the area of the authority:

[*Here list all maintained, grant-maintained, and grant-maintained special schools in the authority's area which provide primary education, or list all such schools which provide secondary education, depending on whether the child requires primary or secondary education. Alternatively, list the required information in a list attached to this notice.*]

7. A list of the non-maintained special schools which make special educational provision for pupils with special educational needs in England and Wales and are approved by the Secretary of State for Education or the Secretary of State for Wales is attached to this notice.

8. A list of the independent schools in England and Wales which are approved by the Secretary of State for Education or the Secretary of State for Wales as suitable for the admission of children for whom statements of special educational needs are maintained is attached to this notice.

9. You are entitled to make representations to the authority about the content of the statement. If you wish to make such representations you must do so not later than 15 days from the date on which you receive this notice, or 15 days from the date on which you last attended a meeting in accordance with the next paragraph, whichever is the later date.

10. You are entitled, not later than 15 days from the date on which you receive this notice, to require the authority to arrange a meeting between you and an officer of the authority at which any part of the statement, or all of it, may be discussed. In particular, any advice on which the statement is based may be discussed.

11. If having attended a meeting in accordance with paragraph 10 above you still disagree with any part of the assessment in question, you may within 15 days of the date of the meeting require the authority to arrange a meeting or meetings to discuss the advice which they consider relevant to the part of

the assessment you disagree with. They will arrange for the person who gave the advice, or some other person whom they think appropriate, to attend the meeting.

12. If at the conclusion of the procedure referred to above the authority serve on you a statement with which you disagree you may appeal to the Special Educational Needs Tribunal against the description of your child's special educational needs, against the special educational provision specified including the school named, or, if no school is named, against that fact.

13. All correspondence with the authority should be addressed to the officer responsible for this case:

[*Here set out name, address and telephone number of case officer, and any reference number which should be quoted.*]

[*Date*]   [*Signature of officer responsible*]

PART B: STATEMENT OF SPECIAL EDUCATIONAL NEEDS

Part 1: Introduction

1. In accordance with section 168 of the Education Act 1993 ('the Act') and the Education (Special Educational Needs) Regulations 1994 ('the Regulations'), the following statement is made by [*here set out name of authority*] ('the authority') in respect of the child whose name and other particulars are mentioned below.

Child

Surname........................	Other names ....
Home address....................	....
....	Sex................................
....	Religion ....
Date of Birth	Home language ....

Child's parent or person responsible

Surname........................	Other names ....
Home address....................	....
....	Relationship to child ....
Telephone No.....................	

2. When assessing the child's special educational needs the authority took into consideration, in accordance with regulation 10 of the Regulations, the representations, evidence and advice set out in the Appendices to this statement.

Part 2: Special educational needs
[*Here set out the child's special educational needs, in terms of the child's learning difficulties which call for special educational provision, as assessed by the authority.*]

Part 3: Special educational provision
OBJECTIVES
[*Here specify the objectives which the special educational provision for the child should aim to meet.*]

EDUCATIONAL PROVISION TO MEET NEEDS AND OBJECTIVES
[*Here specify the special educational provision which the authority consider appropriate to meet the needs specified in Part 2 and to meet the objectives specified in this Part, and in particular specify –*

- (a) any appropriate facilities and equipment, staffing arrangements and curriculum,
- (b) any appropriate modifications to the application of the National Curriculum,
- (c) any appropriate exclusions from the application of the National Curriculum, in detail, and the provision which it is proposed to substitute for any such exclusions in order to maintain a balanced and broadly based curriculum; and
- (d) where residential accommodation is appropriate, that fact].

MONITORING
[*Here specify the arrangements to be made for –*

- (a) regularly monitoring progress in meeting the objectives specified in this Part,
- (b) establishing targets in furtherance to those objectives,
- (c) regularly monitoring the targets referred to in (b),
- (d) regularly monitoring the appropriateness of any modifications to the application of the National Curriculum, and
- (e) regularly monitoring the appropriateness of any provision substituted for exclusions from the application of the National Curriculum.

Here also specify any special arrangements for reviewing this statement.]

Part 4: Placement
[*Here specify –*

- (a) the type of school which the authority consider appropriate for the child and the name of the school for which the parent has expressed a preference or, where the authority are required to specify the name of a school, the name of the school which they consider would be appropriate for the child and should be specified, or
- (b) the provision for his education otherwise than at a school which the authority consider appropriate.]

Part 5: Non-educational needs
[*Here specify the non-educational needs of the child for which the authority consider provision is appropriate if the child is to properly benefit from the special educational provision specified in Part 3.*]

Part 6: Non-educational provision
[*Here specify any non-educational provision which the authority propose to make available or which they are satisfied will be made available by a district health authority, a social services authority or some other body, including the arrangements for its provision. Also specify the objectives of the provision, and the arrangements for monitoring progress in meeting those objectives.*]

_____   _____

Date   *A duly authorised officer of the authority*

Appendix A: Parental representations
[*Here set out any written representations made by the parent of the child under section 167(1)(d) of or paragraph 4(1) of Schedule 10 to the Act and a summary which the parent has accepted as accurate of any oral representations so made or record that no such representations were made.*]

Appendix B: Parental evidence
[*Here set out any written evidence either submitted by the parent of the child under section 167(1)(d) of the Act or record that no such evidence was submitted.*]

Appendix C: Advice from the child's parent
[*Here set out the advice obtained under regulation 6(1)(a).*]

Appendix D: Educational advice
[*Here set out the advice obtained under regulation 6(1)(b).*]

Appendix E: Medical advice
[*Here set out the advice obtained under regulation 6(1)(c).*]

Appendix F: Psychological advice
[*Here set out the advice obtained under regulation 6(1)(d).*]

Appendix G: Advice from the social services authority
[*Here set out the advice obtained under regulation 6(1)(e).*]

Appendix H: Other advice obtained by the authority
[*Here set out the advice obtained under regulation 6(1)(f).*]

EXPLANATORY NOTE

(This Note is not part of the Regulations)

These Regulations relate to the assessment of special educational needs and to statements of such needs under Part III of the Education Act 1993. Part III replaces with modifications the provisions relating to such assessments and statements in the Education Act 1981, and these Regulations replace with modifications the Education (Special Educational Needs) Regulations 1983, which are revoked (regulation 20).

The Regulations make provision for a head teacher to delegate his functions under them generally to a qualified teacher, or in a particular case to the staff member who teaches the child (regulation 3).

The Regulations provide that local education authorities in making an assessment of a child's special educational needs must seek advice from the child's parent, educational advice, medical advice, psychological advice, advice from the social services authority and any other advice which they consider appropriate for the purpose of arriving at a satisfactory assessment (regulation 6). If such advice has been obtained on making a previous assessment within the last 12 months and certain persons are satisfied that it is sufficient, it is not necessary to obtain new advice (regulation 6(5)). Detailed provision is made as to the persons from whom educational, medical and psychological advice must be sought (regulations 7 to 9). It is provided that in making an assessment an authority shall take into consideration representations from the parent, evidence submitted by the parent, and the advice which has been obtained (regulation 10).

The Regulations prescribe the form and content of a notice to be served on a parent with a draft statement of special educational needs, and of a statement of special educational needs (regulations 12 and 13 and Part A and B of the Schedule respectively).

The Regulations also supplement the procedural framework for making an assessment and a statement contained in Part III of the Education Act 1993 and Schedules 9 and 10 thereto. Detailed provision is made for the service of documents by post (regulation 4). They require copies of notices of a local education authority's proposal to make an assessment, their decision to make an assessment or notices of a parent's request for an assessment to be made, to be served on the social services authority, the district health authority and the head teacher of the child's school (regulation 5). Subject to exceptions, they require local education authorities to carry out various steps in making an assessment or a statement within prescribed time limits (regulations 11 and 14 respectively).

Detailed provision is made as to how a review of a statement by a local education authority under section 172 of the Education Act 1993 is to be carried out (regulations 15 to 17). In particular it is provided that where a child attends school where the review is the first review after he has attained the age of 14 the head teacher of his school will obtain advice, the local education authority will chair a meeting, and the authority will prepare a transition plan (regulation 16). In the case of any other review where a child attends school the head teacher of his school will obtain advice, he will chair a meeting and report to the local education authority (regulation 15). Where a child does not attend school provision is made for the local authority to obtain advice, to chair a meeting, and where the review is the first after he attains the age of 14, to prepare a transition plan (regulation 17).

The Regulations provide for the transfer of a statement from one local education authority to another (regulation 18). The duties of the transferor are transferred to the transferee, and within six weeks of the transfer the transferee must serve a notice on the parent informing him of the transfer, whether they propose to make an assessment, and when they propose to review the statement (regulation 18(2) and (3)). It is provided that where it would not be practicable to require the transferee to arrange for the child's attendance at another school until it is possible to amend the statement (regulation 18(5)).

There are restrictions on the disclosure of statements and steps are to be taken to avoid unauthorised persons having access to them (regulation 19).

Detailed provision is made for the transition from the regime imposed by the 1983 Regulations to the regime imposed by these Regulations (regulation 21). In particular if an assessment has been commenced before 1st September 1994 the local education authority may continue to make the assessment under the 1983 Regulations, and may make any statement following the assessment under them as well (regulation 21(2) and (7)). These Regulations, and the time limits they impose, will not apply. However if the assessment is not complete before 1st January 1995 these Regulations will apply to the assessment as if it had been commenced under them on that date (regulation 21(3)).

THE SPECIAL EDUCATIONAL NEEDS TRIBUNAL REGULATIONS 1994: EDUCATION, ENGLAND AND WALES (1994 1910)

Part 1: General
CITATION AND COMMENCEMENT

1. These Regulations may be cited as the Special Educational Needs Tribunal Regulations 1994 and shall come into force on 1st September 1994.
INTERPRETATION

2. In these Regulations, unless the context otherwise requires –

'the 1993 Act' means the Education Act 1993;

'authority' means the local education authority which made the disputed decision;

'child' means the child in respect of whom the appeal is brought;

'disputed decision' means the decision or determination in respect of which the appeal is brought;

'the clerk to the tribunal' means the person appointed by the Secretary of the Tribunal to act in that capacity at one or more hearings;

'hearing' means a sitting of the tribunal duly constituted for the purpose of receiving evidence, hearing addresses and witnesses or doing anything lawfully requisite to enable the tribunal to reach a decision on any question;

'parent' means a parent who has made an appeal to the Special Educational Needs Tribunal under the 1993 Act;

'records' means the records of the Special Educational Needs Tribunal;

'the Secretary of the Tribunal' means the person for the time being acting as the Secretary of the office of the Special Educational Needs Tribunal;

'the tribunal' means the Special Educational Needs Tribunal but where the President has determined pursuant to regulation 4(1) that the jurisdiction of the Special Educational Needs Tribunal is to be exercised by more than one tribunal, it means, in relation to any proceedings, the tribunal to which the proceedings have been referred by the President;

'working day' means any day other than –

    (a) a Saturday, a Sunday, Christmas Day, Good Friday or a day which is a bank holiday within the meaning of the Banking and Financial Deals Act 1971**(d)**;

    (b) a day in August.

MEMBERS OF LAY PANEL

3. No person may be appointed member of the lay panel unless the Secretary of State is satisfied that he has knowledge and experience in respect of –

    (a) children with special educational needs; or

    (b) local government.

ESTABLISHMENT OF TRIBUNALS

4. –(1) Such number of tribunals shall be established to exercise the jurisdiction of the Special Educational Needs Tribunal as the President may from time to time determine.

(2) The tribunals shall sit at such times and in such places as may from time to time be determined by the President.

MEMBERSHIP OF TRIBUNAL

5. –(1) Subject to the provisions of regulation 29(5), the tribunal shall consist of a chairman and two other members.

(2) For each hearing –

    (a) the chairman shall be the President or a person selected from the chairman's panel by the President; and

    (b) the two other members of the tribunal other than the chairman shall be selected from the lay panel by the President.

PROOF OF DOCUMENTS AND CERTIFICATION OF DECISIONS

6. –(1) A document purporting to be a document issued by the Secretary of the Tribunal on behalf of the Special Educational Needs Tribunal shall, unless the contrary is proved, be deemed to be a document so issued.

(2) A document purporting to be certified by the Secretary of the Tribunal to be a true copy of a document containing a decision of the tribunal shall, unless the contrary is proved, be sufficient evidence of matters contained therein.

Part 2: Making an appeal to the tribunal and reply by the authority: (a) the parent
NOTICE OF APPEAL

7. –(1) An appeal to the Special Educational Needs Tribunal shall be made by notice which –

    (a) shall state –

(d) 1971 c.80

> > (i) the name and address of the parent making the appeal;
> > (ii) the name of the child;
> > (iii) that the notice is a notice of appeal;
> > (iv) the name of the authority which made the disputed decision and the date on which the parent was notified of it;
> > (v) the grounds of the appeal;
>
> (b) shall be accompanied (as appropriate) by –
>
> > (i) a copy of the notice of the disputed decision;
> > (ii) a copy of the child's statement of special educational needs; and
>
> (c) may state the name, address and profession of any representative of the parent to whom the tribunal should send replies or notices concerning the appeal instead of to the parent.

(2) The parent shall sign the notice of appeal.

(3) The parent must deliver the notice of appeal to the Secretary of the Tribunal so that it is received no later than the first working day after the expiry of 2 months from the date on which the authority gave him notice, pursuant to the 1993 Act, that he had a right of appeal.

RESPONSE, AMENDMENT OF APPEAL AND DELIVERY OF SUPPLEMENTARY GROUNDS OF APPEAL

8. –(1) If the authority delivers a reply under regulation 12 the parent may deliver a written response to it.

(2) A response under paragraph (1) above must be delivered to the Secretary of the Tribunal not later than 15 working days from the date on which the parent receives a copy of the authority's written reply from the Secretary of the Tribunal.

(3) The parent may in exceptional cases (in addition to delivering a response under paragraph (1) above –

> (a) with the permission of the President, at any time before the hearing; or
>
> (b) with the permission of the tribunal at the hearing itself –

amend the notice of appeal or any response, deliver a supplementary statement of grounds of appeal or amend a supplementary statement of grounds of appeal.

(4) The parent shall delivery a copy of every amendment and supplementary statement made under paragraph (3) above before the hearing to the Secretary of the Tribunal.

WITHDRAWAL OF APPEAL

9. The parent may –

> (a) at any time before the hearing of the appeal withdraw his appeal by sending to the Secretary of the Tribunal a notice signed by him stating that he withdraws his appeal;
>
> (b) at the hearing of the appeal, withdraw his appeal.

FURTHER ACTION BY PARENT

10. –(1) The parent shall supply the Secretary of the Tribunal with the information requested in the enquiry made under regulation 18.

(2) If the parent does not intend to attend or be represented at the hearing, he may, not less than 5 working days before the hearing, send to the Secretary of the Tribunal additional written representations in support of his appeal.

REPRESENTATIVES OF THE PARENT: FURTHER PROVISIONS

11. –(1) Where a parent has not stated the name of a representative in the notice of appeal pursuant to regulation 7(1)(c) he may at any time before the hearing notify the Secretary of the Tribunal of the name, address and profession of a representative to whom the tribunal should send any subsequent documents or notices concerning the appeal instead of to the parent.

(2) Where a parent has stated the name of a representative, whether in the notice of appeal pursuant to regulation 7(1)(c) or pursuant to paragraph (1) above, he may at any time notify the Secretary of the Tribunal –

(a) of the name, address and profession of a new representative of the parent to whom the tribunal should send documents or notices concerning the appeal instead of to the representative previously notified; or

(b) that no person is acting as a representative of the parent and accordingly any subsequent documents or notices concerning the appeal should be sent to the parent himself.

(3) At a hearing, the parent may conduct his case himself (with assistance from one person if he wishes) or may appear and be represented by one person whether or not legally qualified;

Provided that, if the President gives permission before the hearing or the tribunal gives permission at the hearing, the parent may obtain assistance or be represented by more than one person.

(b) The reply by the authority

ACTION BY THE AUTHORITY ON RECEIPT OF A NOTICE OF APPEAL

12. –(1) An authority which receives a copy of a notice of appeal shall deliver to the Secretary of the Tribunal a written reply acknowledging service upon it of the notice of appeal and stating –

(a) whether or not the authority intends to oppose the appeal and, if it does intend to oppose the appeal, the grounds on which it relies; and

(b) the name and profession of the representative of the authority and the address for service of the authority for the purposes of the appeal.

(2) The authority shall include with its reply a statement summarising the facts relating to the disputed decision and, if they are not part of that decision, the reasons for the disputed decision.

(3) Every such reply shall be signed by an officer of the authority who is authorised to sign such documents and shall be delivered to the Secretary of the Tribunal not later than 20 working days after the date on which the copy

of the notice of appeal was received by the authority from the Secretary of the Tribunal.

AMENDMENT OF REPLY BY THE AUTHORITY

13. –(1) The authority, if it has delivered a reply pursuant to regulation 12, may, in exceptional cases –

(a) with the permission of the President at any time before the hearing; or

(b) with the permission of the tribunal at the hearing itself

amend its reply, deliver a supplementary reply or amend a supplementary reply.

(2) The President or, as the case may be, the tribunal may give permission under paragraph (1) above on such terms as he or it thinks fit including the payment of costs or expenses.

(3) The authority shall send a copy of every amendment and supplementary statement made before the hearing to the Secretary of the Tribunal.

NOTICE THAT AN APPEAL IS MISCONCEIVED

14. –(1) Where the authority is of the opinion that an appeal does not lie to, or cannot be entertained by, the Special Educational Needs Tribunal, it may serve a notice to that effect on the Secretary of the Tribunal stating the grounds for such contention and applying for the appeal to be struck out.

(2) The Secretary of the Tribunal shall send a copy of the notice and of any accompanying documents to the parent.

(3) An application under this regulation may be heard by the tribunal as a preliminary point of law or at the beginning of the hearing of the substantive appeal.

FAILURE TO REPLY AND ABSENCE OF OPPOSITION

15. If no reply is received by the Secretary of the Tribunal within the time appointed by regulation 12(3) or if the authority states in writing that it does not resist the appeal, or withdraws its opposition to the appeal, the tribunal may determine the appeal on the basis of the notice of appeal without a hearing or may (without notifying the authority) hold a hearing at which the authority is not represented.

REPRESENTATION AT HEARING AND FURTHER ACTION BY THE AUTHORITY

16. –(1) At a hearing the authority may be represented by one person whether or not legally qualified:

Provided that if the President gives permission before the hearing or the tribunal gives permission at the hearing the authority may be represented by more than one person.

(2) The authority shall supply the Secretary of the Tribunal with the information requested in the enquiry made under regulation 18.

(3) If the authority does not intend to attend or be represented at the hearing it may, not less than 5 working days before the hearing, send to the Secretary of the Tribunal additional written representations in support of its reply.

Part 3: Preparation for a hearing
ACKNOWLEDGEMENT OF APPEAL AND SERVICE OF DOCUMENTS BY THE
SECRETARY OF THE TRIBUNAL

17. –(1) Upon receiving a notice of appeal the Secretary of the Tribunal shall –

(a) enter particulars of it in the records;

(b) send to the parent –

    (i) an acknowledgement of its receipt and a note of the case number entered in the records;

    (ii) a note of the address to which notices and communications to the Special Educational Needs Tribunal or to the Secretary of the Tribunal should be sent; and

    (iii) notification that advice about the appeal procedure may be obtained from the office of the Special Educational Needs Tribunal;

(c) subject to paragraph (5) below, send to the authority –

    (i) a copy of the notice of appeal and any accompanying papers;

    (ii) a note of the address to which notices and communications to the Special Educational Needs Tribunal or to the Secretary of the Tribunal should be sent, and

    (iii) a notice stating the time for replying and the consequences of failure to do so.

(2) Where the Secretary of the Tribunal is of the opinion that, on the basis of the notice of appeal, the parent is asking the Special Educational Needs Tribunal to do something which it cannot, he may give notice to that effect to the parent stating the reasons for his opinion and informing him that the notice of appeal will not be entered in the records unless the parent notifies the Secretary of the Tribunal that he wishes to proceed with it.

(3) An appeal, as respects which a notice has been given in pursuance of paragraph (2) above, shall only be treated as having been received for the purposes of paragraph (1) when the parent notifies the Secretary of the Tribunal that he wishes to proceed with it.

(4) Subject to paragraph (5) below, the Secretary of the Tribunal shall forthwith send a copy of a reply by the authority under regulation 12 and of a response under regulation 8 together with any amendments or supplementary statements, written representations or other documents received from a party, to the other party to the proceedings.

(5) If a notice of appeal, reply by the authority under regulation 12 or response by the parent under regulation 8 is delivered to the Secretary of the Tribunal after the time prescribed by these Regulations, the Secretary of the Tribunal shall defer the sending of the copies referred to in paragraph (1)(c) or (4) above pending a decision by the President as to an extension of the time limit pursuant to regulation 42.

ENQUIRIES BY SECRETARY OF THE TRIBUNAL

18. The Secretary of the Tribunal shall, at any time after he has received the notice of appeal –

(a) enquire of each party –

(i) whether or not the party intends to attend the hearing;

(ii) whether the party wishes to be represented at the hearing in accordance with regulation 11(3) or 16(1) and if so the name of the representative;

(iii) whether the party wishes the hearing to be in public;

(iv) whether the party intends to call witnesses and if so the names of the proposed witnesses; and

(v) whether the party or a witness will require the assistance of an interpreter; and

(b) enquire of the parent whether he wishes any persons (other than a person who will represent him) to attend the hearing if the hearing is to be in private and if so the names of such person.

DIRECTIONS IN PREPARATION FOR A HEARING

19. –(1) the President may at any time give such directions (including the issue of a witness summons) as are provided in this Part of these Regulations to enable the parties to prepare for the hearing or to assist the tribunal to determine the issues.

(2) Directions given pursuant to regulations 21 and 22 may be given on the application of a party or of the President's own motion.

(3) A witness summons issued pursuant to regulation 23 may only be issued on the application of a party.

(4) An application by a party for directions (other than during a hearing) shall be made in writing to the Secretary of the Tribunal and, unless it is accompanied by the written consent of the other party, shall be served by the Secretary of the Tribunal on that other party. If the other party objects to the directions sought, the President shall consider the objection and, if he considers it necessary for the determination of the application, shall give the parties an opportunity of appearing before him.

(5) Directions containing a requirement under this Part of these Regulations shall, as appropriate –

(a) include a statement of the possible consequences for the appeal, as provided by regulation 24, of a party's failure to comply with the requirement within the time allowed by the President; and

(b) contain a reference to the fact that, under section 180(5) of the 1993 Act, any person who without reasonable excuse fails to comply with requirements regarding discovery or inspection of documents, or regarding attendance to give evidence and produce documents, shall be liable on summary conviction to a fine not exceeding level 3 on the standard scale and shall, unless the person to whom the direction is addressed had an opportunity of objecting to the direction, contain a statement to the effect that that person may apply to the President under regulation 20 to vary or set aside the direction.

VARYING OR SETTING ASIDE OF DIRECTIONS

20. Where a person to whom a direction (including any summons) given under this Part of these Regulations is addressed had no opportunity to object to the giving of such direction, he may apply to the President, by notice to the Secretary of the Tribunal, to vary it or set it aside, but the President shall not so do without first notifying the person who applied for the direction and considering any representations made by him.

PARTICULARS AND SUPPLEMENTARY STATEMENTS

21. The President may give directions requiring any party to provide such particulars or supplementary statements as may be reasonably required for the determination of the appeal.

DISCLOSURE OF DOCUMENTS AND OTHER MATERIAL

22. –(1) the President may give directions requiring a party to deliver to the tribunal any document or other material which the tribunal may require and which it is in the power of that party to deliver. The President shall make such provision as he thinks necessary to supply copies of any document obtained under this paragraph to the other party to the proceedings, and it shall be a condition of such supply that that party shall use such a document only for the purposes of the appeal.

(2) The President may grant to a party such discovery or inspection of documents (including the taking of copies) as might be granted by a county court.

SUMMONING OF WITNESSES

23. The President may by summons any person in England and Wales to attend as a witness at a hearing of an appeal at such time and place as may be specified in the summons and at the hearing to answer any questions or produce any documents or other material in his custody or under his control which relate to any matter in question in the appeal:

Provided that –

(a) no person shall be compelled to give any evidence or produce any document or other material that he could not be compelled to give or produce at a trial of an action in a Court of law;

(b) in exercising the powers conferred by this regulation, the President shall take into account the need to protect any matter that relates to intimate personal or financial circumstances or consists of information communicated or obtained in confidence;

(c) no person shall be required to attend in obedience to such a summons unless he has been given at least 5 working days' notice of the hearing or, if less than 5 working days, he has informed the President that he accepts such notice as he has been given; and

(d) no person shall be required in obedience to such a summons to attend and give evidence or to produce any document unless the necessary expenses of his attendance are paid or tendered to him.

FAILURE TO COMPLY WITH DIRECTIONS

24. –(1) If a party has not complied with a direction to it under this Part of these Regulations within the time specified in the direction the tribunal may –

(a) where the party in default is the parent, dismiss the appeal without a hearing;

(b) where the party in default is the authority, determine the appeal without a hearing; or

(c) hold a hearing (without notifying the party in default) at which the party in default is not represented.

(2) In this regulation 'the party in default' means the party which has failed to comply with the direction.

NOTICE OF PLACE AND TIME OF HEARING AND ADJOURNMENTS

25. –(1) Subject to the provisions of regulation 26, the Secretary of the Tribunal shall, with due regard to the convenience of the parties, fix the time and place of the hearing and, not less than 10 working days before the date so fixed (or such shorter time as the parties agree, send to each party a notice that the hearing is to be at such time and place.

(2) the Secretary of the Tribunal shall include in or with the notice of hearing –

(a) information and guidance, in a form approved by the President, as to attendance at the hearing of the parties and witnesses, the bringing of documents, and the right of representation or assistance as provided by regulation 11(3) or 16(1); and

(b) a statement explaining the possible consequences of non-attendance and of the right of –

(i) a parent; and

(ii) the authority, if it has presented a reply,

who does not attend and is not represented, to make representations in writing.

(4) The tribunal may alter the time and place of any hearing and the Secretary of the Tribunal shall give the parties not less than 5 working days (or such shorter time as the parties agree) notice of the altered hearing date:

Provided that any altered hearing date shall not (unless the parties agree) be before the date notified under paragraph (1).

(5) The tribunal may from time to time adjourn the hearing and, if the time and place of the adjourned hearing are announced before the adjournment, no further notice shall be required.

Part 4: Determination of appeals
POWER TO DETERMINE AN APPEAL WITHOUT A HEARING

26. –(1) The tribunal may –

(a) if the parties so agree in writing; or

(b) in the circumstances described in regulations 15 and 24,

determine an appeal or any particular issue without a hearing.

(2) The provisions of regulation 28(2) shall apply in respect of the determination of an appeal, or any particular issue, under this regulation.

HEARINGS TO BE IN PRIVATE: EXCEPTIONS

27. –(1) A hearing by the tribunal shall be in private unless –

(a) both the parent and the authority request that the hearing be in public; or

(b) the tribunal orders that he hearing should be in public.

(2) The following persons (as well as the parties and their representatives) shall be entitled to attend the hearing of an appeal, even though it is in private –

(a) any person named by the parent in response to the enquiry under regulation 18(b) unless the President has determined that any such person shall not be entitled to attend the hearing and notified the parent accordingly;

(b) a parent of the child who is not a party to the appeal;

(c) the clerk to the tribunal and the Secretary of the Tribunal;

(d) the President and any member of the chairmen's or lay panel (when not sitting as members of the tribunal);

(e) a member of the Council on Tribunals;

(f) any person undergoing training as a member of the chairmen's or lay panel or as a clerk to the tribunal;

(g) any person acting on behalf of the President in the training or supervision of clerks to tribunals;

(h) an interpreter.

(3) The tribunal, with the consent of the parties or their representatives actually present, may permit any other person to attend the hearing of an appeal which is held in private.

(4) Without prejudice to any other powers it may have, the tribunal may exclude from the hearing, or part of it, any person whose conduct has disrupted or is likely, in the opinion of the tribunal, to disrupt the hearing.

(5) For the purposes of arriving at its decision a tribunal shall, and for the purposes of discussing any question of procedure may, notwithstanding anything contained in these Regulations, order all persons to withdraw from the sitting of the tribunal other than the members of the tribunal or any of the persons mentioned in paragraph (2)(c) to (f) above.

(6) Except as provided in paragraph (7) below none of the persons mentioned in paragraph (2) or (3) above shall, save in the case of the clerk to the tribunal or an interpreter as their respective duties require, take any part in the hearing or (where entitled or permitted to remain) in the deliberations of the tribunal.

(7) The tribunal may permit a parent of the child who is not a party to the appeal to address the tribunal on the subject matter of the appeal.

FAILURE OF PARTIES TO ATTEND HEARING

28. –(1) If a party fails to attend or be represented at a hearing of which he has been duly notified, the tribunal may –

(a) unless it is satisfied that there is sufficient reason for such absence, hear and determine the appeal in the party's absence; or

(b) adjourn the hearing,

and may make such order as to costs and expenses as it thinks fit.

(2) Before disposing of an appeal in the absence of a party, the tribunal shall consider any representations in writing submitted by that party in response to the notice of hearing and, for the purpose of this regulation the notice of appeal, any reply by the authority under regulations 12 or 13 and any response by the parent under regulation 8 shall be treated as representations in writing.

PROCEDURE AT HEARING

29. –(1) At the beginning of the hearing the chairman shall explain the order of proceeding which the tribunal proposes to adopt.

(2) The tribunal shall conduct the hearing in such manner as it considers most suitable to the clarification of the issues and generally to the just handling of the proceedings; it shall, so far as appears to it appropriate, seek to avoid formality in its proceedings.

(3) The tribunal shall determine the order in which the parties are heard and the issues determined.

(4) The tribunal may, if it is satisfied that it is just and reasonable to do so, permit a party to rely on grounds not stated in his notice of appeal or, as the case may be, his reply or response and to adduce any evidence not presented to the authority before or at the time it took the disputed decision.

(5) If after the commencement of any hearing a member of the tribunal other than the chairman is absent, the hearing may, with the consent of the parties, be conducted by the other two members and in that event the tribunal shall be deemed to be properly constituted and the decision of the tribunal shall be taken by those two members.

EVIDENCE AT HEARING

30. –(1) In the course of the hearing the parties shall be entitled to give evidence, to call witnesses, to question any witnesses and to address the tribunal both on the evidence and generally on the subject matter of the appeal:

Provided that neither party shall be entitled to call more than two witnesses to give evidence orally (in addition to any witnesses whose attendance is required pursuant to paragraph (2) below) unless the President has given permission before the hearing or the tribunal gives permission at the hearing.

(2) Evidence before the tribunal may be given orally or by written statement, but the tribunal may at any stage of the proceedings require the personal attendance of any maker of any written statement.

(3) The tribunal may receive evidence of any fact which appears to the tribunal to be relevant.

(4) The tribunal may require any witness to give evidence on oath or affirmation, and for that purpose there may be administered an oath or affirmation in due form, or may require any evidence given by written statement to be given by affidavit.

DECISION OF THE TRIBUNAL

31. –(1) A decision of the tribunal may be taken by a majority and where the tribunal is constituted by two members only under regulation 29(5) the chairman shall have a second or casting vote.

(2) The decision of the tribunal may be given orally at the end of the hearing or reserved and, in any event, whether there has been a hearing or not, shall be recorded forthwith in a document which, save in the case of a decision by consent, shall also contain, or have annexed to it, a statement of the reasons (in summary form) for the tribunal's decision, and each such document shall be signed and dated by the chairman.

(3) Neither a decision given orally nor the document referred to in paragraph (2) above shall contain any reference to the decision being by majority (if that be the case) or to any opinion of a minority.

(4) Every decision of the tribunal shall be entered in the records.

(5) As soon as may be the Secretary of the Tribunal shall send a copy of the document referred to in paragraph (2) above to each party, accompanied by guidance, in a form approved by the President, about the circumstances in which there is a right to appeal against a tribunal decision and the procedure to be followed.

(6) Every decision shall be treated as having been made on the date on which a copy of the document recording it is sent to the parent (whether or not the decision has been previously announced at the end of the hearing).

REVIEW OF THE TRIBUNAL'S DECISION

32. –(1) If, on the application of a party to the Secretary of the Tribunal or of its own motion, the tribunal is satisfied that –

(a) its decision was wrongly made as a result of an error on the part of the tribunal staff;

(b) a party, who was entitled to be heard at a hearing but failed to appear or be represented, had good and sufficient reason for failing to appear; or

(c) the interests of justice require,

the tribunal may review and, by certificate under the chairman's hand, set aside or vary the relevant decision.

(2) An application for the purposes of paragraph (1) above may be made immediately following the decision at the hearing. If an application is not made at the hearing, it shall be made not later than 10 working days after the date on which the decision was sent to the parties, and shall be in writing stating the grounds in full. When the tribunal proposes to review its decision of its own motion, it shall serve notice of that proposal on the parties within the same period.

(3) An application for the purposes of paragraph (1) above may be refused by the President, or by the chairman of the tribunal which decided the case, if in his opinion it has no reasonable prospect of success.

(4) If the application is not refused under paragraph (3) above, the parties shall have an opportunity to be heard on any application or proposal for review under this regulation and the review shall be determined by the tribunal which decided the case or, where it is not practicable for it to be heard by that tribunal, by a tribunal appointed by the President; and if, having reviewed the decision, the decision is set aside, the tribunal shall substitute such decision as it thinks fit or order a rehearing before either the same or a differently constituted tribunal.

(5) If any decision is set aside or varied under this regulation or altered in any way by order of a superior court, the Secretary of the Tribunal shall alter the entry in the records to conform with the chairman's certificate or order of a superior court and shall notify the parties accordingly.

REVIEW OF THE PRESIDENT'S DECISION

33. –(1) If, on the application of a party to the Secretary of the Tribunal or of his own motion the President is satisfied that –

    (a) a decision by him was wrongly made as a result of an error on the part of the tribunal staff; or

    (b) the interests of justice require,

the President may review and set aside the relevant decision of his.

(2) An application for the purposes of paragraph (1) shall be made not later than 10 working days after the date on which the party making the application was notified of the decision and shall be in writing stating the grounds in full. Where the President proposes to review his decision of his own motion he shall serve notice of that proposal on the parties within the same period.

(3) The parties shall have an opportunity to be heard on any application or proposal for review under this regulation and the review shall be determined by the President.

(4) If any decision is set aside or varied under this regulation the Secretary of the Tribunal shall alter the entry in the records and shall notify the parties accordingly.

ORDERS FOR COSTS AND EXPENSES

34. –(1) The tribunal shall not normally make an order in respect of costs and expenses, but may, subject to paragraph (2) below, make such an order –

    (a) against a party (including any party who has withdrawn his appeal or reply) if it is of the opinion that that party has acted frivolously or vexatiously or that his conduct in making, pursuing or resisting an appeal was wholly unreasonable;

    (b) against an authority which has not delivered a written reply under regulation 12; or

    (c) against the authority, where it considers that the disputed decision was wholly unreasonable.

(2) Any order in respect of costs and expenses may be made –

(a) as respects any costs or expenses incurred, or any allowances paid; or

(b) as respects the whole, or any part, of any allowance (other than allowances paid to members of tribunals) paid by the Secretary of State under section 180(3) of the 1993 Act to any person for the purposes of, or in connection with, his attendance at the tribunal.

(3) No order shall be made under paragraph (1) above against a party without first giving that party an opportunity of making representations against the making of the order.

(4) An order under paragraph (1) above may require the party against whom it is made to pay the other party either a specified sum in respect of the costs and expenses incurred by that other party in connection with the proceedings or the whole or part of such costs as taxed (if not otherwise agreed).

(5) Any costs required by an order under this regulation to be taxed may be taxed in the county court according to such of the scales prescribed by the county court rules for proceedings in the county court as shall be directed in the order.

Part 5: Additional powers of and provisions relating to the tribunal
TRANSFER OF PROCEEDINGS

35. Where it appears to the President that an appeal pending before a tribunal could be determined more conveniently in another tribunal he may at any time, upon the application of a party or of his own motion, direct that the said proceedings be transferred so as to be determined in that other tribunal:

Provided that no such direction shall be given unless notice has been sent to all parties concerned giving them an opportunity to show cause why such a direction should not be given.

MISCELLANEOUS POWERS OF THE TRIBUNAL

36. –(1) Subject to the provisions of the 1993 Act and these Regulations, a tribunal may regulate its own procedure.

(2) A tribunal may, if it thinks fit, if both parties agree in writing upon the terms of a decision to be made by the tribunal, decide accordingly.

POWER TO STRIKE OUT

37. –(1) The tribunal may, on the application of the President or the authority, at any stage of the proceedings order that an appeal should be struck out –

(a) on the grounds that it is not within the jurisdiction of the Special Educational Needs Tribunal;

(b) on the grounds that the appeal or the notice of appeal is scandalous, frivolous or vexatious; or

(c) for want of prosecution.

(2) Before the tribunal makes an order under paragraph (1) above, the Secretary of the Tribunal shall give to the parent a notice inviting

representations and the tribunal shall consider any representations duly made. If the parent does not request an opportunity to make oral representations, the Tribunal need not hold a hearing.

(3) The president may, if he thinks fit, at any stage of the proceedings order that a reply, response or statement should be struck out or amended on the grounds that it is scandalous, frivolous or vexatious.

(4) Before making an order under paragraph (3) above, the President shall give to the party against whom he proposes to make the order a notice inviting representations and shall consider any representations duly made.

(5) For the purposes of paragraphs (2) and (4) above –

(a) a notice inviting representations must inform the recipient that he may, within a period (not being less than 5 working days) specified in the notice, either make written representations or request an opportunity to make oral representations;

(b) representations are duly made if –

(i) in the case of written representations, they are made within the period so specified; and

(ii) in the case of oral representations, the party proposing to make them has requested an opportunity to do so within the period so specified.

POWER TO EXERCISE POWERS OF THE PRESIDENT AND CHAIRMAN

38. –(1) An act required or authorised by these Regulations to be done by the President may be done by a member of the chairman's panel authorised by the President.

(2) Where, pursuant to paragraph (1) above, a member of the chairman's panel carries out the function under regulation 5(2) of selecting the chairman of a tribunal, he may select himself.

(3) Where, pursuant to paragraph (1) above a member of the chairman's panel makes a decision, regulation 33 shall apply in relation to that decision taking the reference in that regulation to the President as a reference to the member of the chairman's panel by whom the decision was taken.

(4) Subject to regulation 40(5) in the event of the death or incapacity of the chairman following the decision of the tribunal in any matter, the functions of the chairman for the completion of the proceedings, including any review of the decision, may be exercised by the President or any member of the chairman's panel.

THE SECRETARY OF THE TRIBUNAL

39. A function of the Secretary of the Tribunal may be performed by another member of the staff of the tribunal authorised for the purpose of carrying out that function by the President.

IRREGULARITIES

40. –(1) An irregularity resulting from failure to comply with any provisions of these Regulations or of any direction of the tribunal before the tribunal has reached its decision shall not of itself render the proceedings void.

(2) Where any such irregularity comes to the attention of the tribunal, the tribunal may, and shall, if it considers that any person may have been prejudiced by the irregularity, give such directions as it thinks just before reaching its decision to cure or waive the irregularity.

(3) Clerical mistakes in any document recording a decision of the tribunal or a direction or decision of the President produced by or on behalf of the tribunal or errors arising in such documents from accidental slips or omissions may at any time be corrected by the chairman or the President (as the case may be) by certificate under his hand.

(4) the Secretary of the Tribunal shall as soon as may be send a copy of any corrected document containing reasons for the tribunal's decision, to each party.

(5) Where by these Regulations a document is required to be signed by the chairman but by reason of death or incapacity the chairman is unable to sign such a document, it shall be signed by the other members of the tribunal, who shall certify that the chairman is unable to sign.

METHOD OF SENDING, DELIVERING OR SERVING NOTICES AND DOCUMENTS

41. –(1) A notice given under these Regulations shall be in writing and where under these Regulations provision is made for a party to notify the Secretary of the Tribunal of any matter he shall do so in writing.

(2) All notices and documents required by these Regulations to be sent or delivered to the Secretary of the Tribunal or the tribunal may be sent by post or by facsimile or delivered to or at the office of the Special Educational Needs Tribunal or such other office as may be notified by the Secretary of the Tribunal to the parties.

(3) All notices and documents required or authorised by these Regulations to be sent or given to any person mentioned in sub-paragraph (a) or (b) below may (subject to paragraph (5) below) either be sent by first class post or by facsimile or delivered to or at –

  (a) in the case of a notice or document directed to a party –
    (i) his address for service specified in the notice of appeal or in a written reply or in a notice under paragraph (4) below, or
    (ii) if no address for service has been so specified, his last known address; and

  (b) in the case of a notice or document directed to any person other than a party, his address or place of business or if such a person is a corporation, the corporation's registered or principal office and if sent or given to the authorised representative of a party shall be deemed to have been sent or given to that party.

(4) A party may at any time by notice to the Secretary of the Tribunal change his address for service under these Regulations.

(5) The recorded delivery service shall be used instead of the first class post for service of a summons issued under regulation 23 requiring the attendance of a witness.

(6) A notice or document sent by the Secretary of the Tribunal by post in accordance with these Regulations, and not returned, shall be taken to have been delivered to the addressee on the second working day after it was posted.

(7) A notice or document sent by facsimile shall be taken to have been delivered when it is received in legible form.

(8) Where for any sufficient reason service of any document or notice cannot be effected in the manner prescribed under this regulation, the President may dispense with service or make an order for substituted service in such manner as he may deem fit and such service shall have the same effect as service in the manner prescribed under this regulation.

EXTENSION OF TIME

42. –(1) Where, pursuant to any provision of these Regulations anything is required to be done by a party within a period of time the President may, on the application of the party in question, in exceptional circumstances extend any period of time.

(2) Where a period of time has been extended pursuant to paragraph (1) above any reference in these Regulations to that period of time shall be construed as a reference to the period of time as so extended.

PARENT'S REPRESENTATIVE

43. Where, pursuant to regulation 7(1)(c) or 11(1) or (2)(a) a parent has stated the name of a representative, and has not subsequently notified the Secretary of the Tribunal pursuant to regulation 11(2)(b) that no person is acting as a representative, any reference in Part 3, 4 or 5 of these Regulations (however expressed) to sending documents to, or giving notice to, the parent shall be construed as a reference to sending documents to or giving notice to the representative and any such reference to sending documents to or giving notice to a party or the parties shall in the context of the parent be likewise construed as a reference to sending documents to, or giving notice to the representative.

Explanatory note
(This note is not part of the Regulations)

These Regulations make provision in relation to the establishment of and regulate the procedure of the Special Educational Needs Tribunal established by section 177 of the Education Act 1993.

Part 1 contains general provisions including provisions as to the members of the lay panel and the establishment of tribunals to exercise the jurisdiction of the Special Educational Needs Tribunal. Part 2 contains provisions relating to the making of an appeal to the tribunal and the reply by the local education authority. Part 3 contains provisions relating to the preparation for the hearing. Part 4 contains provisions relating to the determination of appeals. Part 5 contains additional powers of, and provisions relating to, the tribunal.

Charities and Voluntary Associations

In the first part of this section organisations offering general help and advice are given. In part two are the societies catering for specific disabilities.

GENERAL

Advisory Centre for Education (ACE)
Unit 1B Aberdeen Studios
22–24 Highbury Grove
London N5 2EA
(0171 354 8321)

Centre for Studies on Inclusive
Education (CSIE)
1 Redland Close
Elm Lane, Redland
Bristol BS6 6UE
(0117 923 8450)

The Childrens Society
Edward Rudolph House
Margery Street
London WC1X OJL
(0171 837 4299)

Contact-a-Family
170 Tottenham Court Road
London W1P 0HA
(0171 383 3555)
Publishes a loose-leaf medical directory of Advice and Support Groups for specific conditions.

DIAL UK
Park Lodge
St Catherine's Hospital
Tickhill Road
Doncaster DN4 8QN
(01302 310123)

Disability Alliance
1st Floor East
Universal House
88–94 Wentworth Street
London E1 7SA
(0171 247 8763)

Disability Law Service (Network)
Room 241 2nd Floor
49–51 Bedford Row
London WC1R 4LR
(0171 831 8031) (Advice service)

Family Fund
Joseph Rowntree Memorial Trust
PO BOX 50
York YO1 1UY
(01904 621115)
Information and advice about educating children with special needs within ordinary schools.

Greater London Association For
Disabled People (GLAD)
336 Brixton Road
London SW9 7AA
(0171 274 0107)

I CAN
Barbican City Gate
1–3 Dufferin Street
London EC1Y 8NA
(0171 374 4422)
I CAN is a children's charity for children with speech and language disorders and sufferers of asthma and eczema.

In Touch
10 Norman Road
Sale
Cheshire M33 3DF
(0161 905 2440)
(information and contacts for rare handicapping conditions)

IPSEA (Independant Panel for
Special Education Advice)
22 Warren Hill Road
Woodbridge
Suffolk IP12 4DU
(01394 382814)
Consists of independent experts who give advice to parents.

MIND (National Association for
Mental Health)
Granta House, 15–19 Broadway
Stratford
London E15 4BQ
(0181 519 2122)

National Association of Toy and
Leisure Libraries
68 Churchway
London NW1 1LT
(0171 387 9592)

National Library for the
Handicapped Child
Wellington House
Wellington Road
Wokingham
Berks RG11 1XS
(01734 89110)

National Portage Association
4 Clifton Road
Winchester
Hants
(01962 860148)
(Work with parents of young
handicapped children)

Physically Handicapped and Able
Bodied (PHAB)
12–14 London Road
Croydon
Surrey CRO 2TA
(0181 667 9443)

Pre-school Playgroup Association
61–63 Kings Cross Road
London WC1X 9LL
(0171 833 0991)

Royal Association for Disability and
Rehabilitation (RADAR)
12 City Forum
250 City Road
London EC1V 8AF
(0171 250 3222)

Royal Society for Mentally
Handicapped Children and Adults
(MENCAP)
123 Golden Lane
London EC1Y ORT
(0171 454 0454)
MENCAP London Division Early
Years project 115 Golden Lane, London
EC1Y OTJ publishes INTERLINK: a
London directory of services for fami-
lies and their young children with spe-
cial needs.

National Council for Voluntary
Organisations (NCVO)
Regents Wharf
8 All Saints Street
London N1 9RL
(0171 713 6161)

Young Minds
22a Boston Place
London NW1 6ER
(0171 724 7262)

SOCIETIES CATERING FOR SPECIFIC CONDITIONS
AIDS
National Aids Helplines Call freephone (0800 567 123) 24 hour personal
advice and discussion. Call freephone
(0800 555 777) for National helpline
publicity pack, free leaflets and book-
lets, and an up-to-date list of literature.

Asthma
The National Asthma Campaign
Providence House
Providence Place
London N1 ONT
(0171 226 2260)

Ataxia
Ataxia
Copse Edge
Thursley Road
Elstead
Godlaming
Surrey GU8 6DJ
(01252 702864)

Autism
National Autistic Society
276 Willesden Lane
London NW2 5RB
(0181 451 1114)

Blind and partially sighted
National Federation of the Blind of
the UK
Unity House
Smyth Street
Westgate, Wakefield
W Yorkshire WF1 1ER
(01924 291313)
National Federation of Families with
Visually Impaired Children (LOOK)

Judith Gilboy
The National Office
Queen Alexandra College
49 Court Oak Road
Birmingham B17 9TG
(0121 428 5038)
Facilitates parents' groups and parents
enhancing the education, welfare and
leisure opportunities of visually impaired children.

Royal National Institute for The Blind
224 Great Portland Street
London W1N 6AA
(0171 388 1266)

Bone-marrow disease,
The Anthony Nolan Bone Marrow
Trust
Unit 2
Heathgate Buildings
75–87 Agincourt Road
London NW3 2NT
(0171 284 1234)

Brain Damage
Association for Brain-Damaged
Children
Clifton House
3 St Paul's Road
Foleshill
Coventry CV6 5DE
(01203 665450)

Brittle Bones
Brittle Bones Society
Ward 8
Strathmartine Hospital
Strathmartine
DD3 OPG
(01382 667603)

Cerebral Palsy
The Spastics Society
12 Park Crescent
London W1N 4EQ
(0171 636 5020/0800 626216)

Scottish Council for Spastics
11 Corstophine Road
Edinburgh EH12 6HP
(0131 337 9876)

Chest and Heart
The Stroke Association,
CHSA House,
White Cross Street
London EC1Y 8JJ
(0171 490 7999)

Clumsiness
Dyspraxia Trust
8 West Alley
Hitchin
Hertfordshire SG5 1EG
(01462 454986)

Colitis and Crohn's
National Association for Colitis and
Crohn's Disease
PO Box 205
St Albans
Hertfordshire AL1 1AB
(01727 844296)

Cystic Fibrosis
Cystic Fibrosis Research Trust
5 Blyth Road
Bromley
Kent BR1 3RS
(0181 464 7211)

Deafness
Breakthrough Trust
Charles W Gillett Centre
998 Bristol Road
Selly Oak
Birmingham B29 6LE
(0121 472 6447)
London Office (0181 853 5661)

British Deaf Association
38 Victoria Place
Carlisle CA1 1HV
(01228 48844)

National Aural Group (NAG),
18 Kings Avenue,
Marcham, Abingdon,
Oxon OX13 6QA
(01865 391492)
A nationwide group of teachers and
parents of deaf children providing
wide-ranging support, information
and advice to help parents help their
deaf children.

National Deaf Children's Society,
45 Hereford Road
London W2 5AH
(0171 229 9272)

Royal National Institute For The Deaf
105 Gower Street
London WC1E 6AH
(0171 387 8033)

Friends for the Young Deaf
FYD Communication Centre
East Court Mansion
Council Offices
College Lane
East Grinstead
West Sussex
(01342 323444)

Deaf/Blind
National Deaf/Blind and Rubella
Association (SENSE)
11–13 Clifton Terrace
London N4 3SR
(0171 272 7774)

Diabetes
British Diabetic Association,
10 Queen Anne Street
London W1M OBD
(0171 323 1531)

Down's Syndrome
Down's Syndrome Association
155 Mitcham Road
London SW17 9PG
(0181 682 4001)

Dyslexia
British Dyslexia Association
98 London Road
Reading
Berkshire RG1 5AU
(01734 668271)

Dyslexia Institute
152 Buckingham Palace Road
London SW1W 9TR
(071 730 8890)

Eczema
National Eczma Society
4 Tavistock Place
London W1CH 9RA
(0171 388 4097)

Epilepsy
Epilepsy Helpline
0800 309030

British Epilepsy Association
Anstey House, 40 Hanover Square
Leeds LS3 1BE
(0113 243 9390)

Epilepsy Association of Scotland
48 Govan Road
Glasgow G51 1JL
(0141 427 4911)

Fragile X Syndrome
Fragile X Society, Mrs Lesley Walker
53 Winchelsea Lane
Hastings
East Sussex TN35 4LG
(01424 81347)

Haemophilia
Haemophilia Society
123 Westminster Bridge Road
London SE1 7HR
(0171 928 2020)

Huntingdon's Disease
Huntingdon's Disease Association
108 Battersea High Street
London SW1 3HP
(0171 223 7000)

Hyperactivity
Hyperactive Children's Support
Group
71 Whyke Lane
Chichester
Sussex PO19 2LD
(01903 725182)

Leukaemia
Leukaemia Care Society
14 Kingfisher Court
Venny Bridge, Pinhoe
Exeter
Devon EX4 8JN
(01392 464848)

ME (Myalgic Encephalomyelitis)
ME Association
Stanhope House
High Street
Stanford-le-Hope
Essex SS17 0HA
(01375 642466)

ME Action Campaign
PO Box 1302
Wells
Somerset BA5 2NE
(01749 670799)

Meningitis
National Meningitis Trust
Fern House
Bath Road
Stroud
Gloucestershire GL5 3TJ
(01453 751738)

Mental Impairment
MENCAP (Royal Society for Mentally
Handicapped Children and Adults)
123 Golden Lane
London EC1Y ORT
(0171 454 0454)

Rathbone Society
1st Floor
Princess House
105–107 Princess Street
Manchester M25 5TU
(0161 236 5358)

Scottish Society for the Mentally
Handicapped
7 Buchanan Street
Glasgow G1 3HL
(0141 226 4541)

Motability
Motability
Gate House
West Gate
The High
Harlow
Essex CM10 1HR
(01279 635666)

Multiple Sclerosis
Federation of MS Therapy Centres
Unit 4
Murdock Road
Bedford MK41 7PD
(01234 325781)

Multiple Scelerosis Society of GB and
Northern Ireland
25 Effie Road
London SW6 1EE
(0171 736 6267)

Muscular Dystrophy
Muscular Dystrophy Group of GB
7–11 Prescott Place
London SW4 6BS
(0171 720 8055)

Physical Disability
Handicapped Adventure Playground
Association
Fulham Palace
Bishops Avenue
London SW6 6EA
(0171 736 4443)

RADAR (Royal Association for
Disablement and Rehabilitation)
12 City Forum
250 City Road
London EC1V 8AF
(0171 250 3222)

REACH (Arm and hand deficient)
Mrs Sue Stokes
12 Wilson Way
Earls Barton
Northants NN6 ONZ
(01604 811041)

STEPS (Leg deficient)
15 Statham Close
Lymm
Cheshire WA13 9NN
(01925 757525)

Spinal Injuries Association
Newport House
76 St James Lane
London N10 3DF
(0181 444 2121)
A self-help group for children and
adults with spinal cord children.

Prader-Willi Syndrome
Prader-Willi Syndrome Association
30 Follet Drive
Abbots Langley
Herts WD5 OLP
(01923 674543)

Restricted Growth
Restricted Growth Association
PO Box 18
Rugeley
Staffordshire
WS15 2GH
(01889 576571)

Child Growth Foundation
2 Mayfield Avenue
London W4 1PW
(0181 994 7625)

Retinitis Pigmentosa
British Retinis Pigmentosa Society
(RPS)
PO Box 350
Buckingham MK18 5EL
(01280 860363)

Rett Syndrome
Rett Syndrome's Association UK
Christine Freeman
29 Carlton Road
London N11 3EX
(0181 361 5161)

Sickle Cell Anaemia
Sickle Cell Society
54 Station Road
London NW10 4UA
(0181 961 7795)

Speech and Language Disorders
AFASIC (Association for all Speech
Impaired Children)
347 Central Markets
London EC1 9NH
(0171 236 3632)

Spina Bifida and Hydrocephalus
Association for Spina Bifida and
Hydrocephalus
Asbah House, 42 Park Road
Peterborough
Cambs PE1 2UQ
(01733 555988)

Spinal Injuries
Spinal Injuries Association
Newport House, 76 St James Lane
London N10 3DF
(0181 444 2121)

Tuberous Sclerosis
Tuberous Sclerosis Association of GB
Mrs Janet Medcalf
Little Barnsley Farm
Milton Road
Catshill
Bromsgrove
Worcs
(01527 871898)

Vaccine Damage
Association of Parents of Vaccine
Damaged Children
Mrs R Fox
2 Church Street
Shipston-on-Stour
Warwickshire CV36 4AP
(01608 661595)

Self Help
More and more areas have their own
self help groups run by and for handicapped people and their parents, who
may produce their own local guides to
services and run advice centres. If there
is one in your area you should be able
to get the address from the Social Services, the local council of Voluntary
Services or the local press.

Contact-a-Family
170 Tottenham Court Road
London W1P 0HA
(0171 383 3555)
Has links with over 9000 independant
self help/mutual support groups and
contacts throughout the country. Of-
fers support and advice to existing
groups, and to parents and professional workers who wish to start a
group in their neighbourhood.

Independent Special Educational
Needs Resource Centre and Helpline
Rosie Johnson
112 Grove Park
Knutsford
Cheshire WA16 8QD
(01565 632666)

Network 81
Co-ordinator – Penny Platt
1–7 Woodfield Terrace
Stanstead
Essex CM24 8AJ
(01279 647415)
A national network of support groups
of parents of children who have special
educational needs.

Parents in Partnership (PiP)
Unit 2
Ground Floor
70 South Lambeth Road
London SW8 1RL
(0171 735 7735)
Assistance to parents of children with
special educational needs with the
stamenting procedures under the education act 1981. Operates in the Greater
London area.

Computer Assistance
ACE (Aids to Communication in
Education)
Ormerod School
Waynflete Road
Headington
Oxford OX3 8DD
(01865 63508)
Assesses children with communic-
ation and learning difficulties.

ACE Access Centre
1 Broadbent Road
Watersheddings
Oldham
Lancashire OL1 4HU
(0161 627 1358)

CENMAC (Centre for Micro-assisted
Communication)
Charlton Park School
Charlton Park Road
London SE7 8HX
(0181 316 7589)
Assesses children and young people
with communication difficulties re-
sulting from motor impairment.

National Access Centre
Hereward College of Further
Education
Bramston Crescent, Tile Hill Lane
Coventry CV4 9SW
(01203 461231)

Equipment
Disabled Living Foundation
380–384 Harrow Road
London W9 2HU
(0171 289 6111)
Permanent exhibition of aids and information service of many aspects of
life for disabled people. By appointment only.

Educational Organisations
Campaign for State Education
(CASE), Secretary
158 Durham Road
London SW20 ODG
(0181 944 8206)
A pressure group of parents seeking to
improve the state education system for
all.

Centre for Studies on Inclusive
Education
1 Redland Close
Elm Lane, Redland
Bristol BS6 6UE
(0117 923 8450)

National Association for the
Education of Sick Children
Open School
18 Victoria Park Square
London E2 9PF
(0181 980 6263)

National Association for Special
Educational Needs (NASEN)
Central Office
York House
Exhall Grange
Wheelwright Lane
Coventry CV7 9HP
(01203 362414)

An amalgamation of National Association for Remedial Education and National Council for Special Education.

Special Education Consortium
c/o Council for Disabled Children
8 Wakley Street
London EC1V 7QE
(0171 843 6000)

Further Education
The National Bureau for Students
with Disabilities (SKILL)
336 Brixton Road
London SW9 7AA
(0171 274 0565)
Provides help and advice on further
and higher education
(Nationwide telephone information
and advice services)

Government Departments and Other Official Bodies

GOVERNMENT DEPARTMENTS AND OTHER OFFICIAL BODIES

Specific enquiries on special education should be addressed to: **Special Education Division,** Department of Education, Sanctuary Buildings, Great Smith Street, London SW1P 3BT (0171 925 5000).

WHERE TO FIND OUT MORE

Department of Education (DOE), Sanctuary Buildings, Great Smith Street, London SW1P 3BT (0171 925 5000).

Welsh Office, Education Department, Phase 2, Government Buildings, Ty Glas Road, Llanishen, Cardiff CF4 5NE (01222 761 456).

Department of Health (DOH), Skipton House, 80 London Road, London SE1 6LW (0171 210 3000).

Council on Tribunals, 22 Kingsway, London WC2B 6LE (0171 936 7045).

Equal Opportunities Commission (EOC), Overseas House, Quay Street, Manchester M3 3HN (0161 833 9244).

Commission for Racial Equality (CRE), Elliot House, 10/12 Allington Street, London SW1E 5EH (0171 828 7022).

Children's Legal Centre, 20 Compton Terrace, London N1 2UN (0171 359 6251).

Law Centres Federation, Duchess House, 18 Warren Street, London W1P 5DB (0171 387 8570).

Centre for Studies on Integration in Education (CSIE), 1 Redland Close Elm Lane, Redland, Bristol BS6 6UE. (0117 923 8450).

List of Cases

Index